A GUIDE TO GARDENS OF NEW ENGLAND

Y0-BCL-424

A GUIDE TO GARDENS OF NEW ENGLAND

OPEN TO THE PUBLIC

BY NICHOLAS ZOOK

1973

BARRE PUBLISHERS

BARRE, MASSACHUSETTS

For all the dedicated gardeners of New England, who brighten our world with their gardens.

⁂

Photographs are by the author except for those which are reproduced through the courtesy of the following: frontispiece, Connecticut Development Commission; page 19, Connecticut College; pages 21 and 23, Arnold Arboretum; page 33, Christopher Ayres, Maine Audubon Society; page 55, Arthur Griffin; page 64, Maine Dept. of Economic Development; page 88, Old Sturbridge Village; page 93, The Preservation Society of Newport County, Rhode Island.

⁂

FRONTISPIECE: THIS SMALL BUILDING IN LITCHFIELD, CONNECTICUT, WAS THE FIRST LAW SCHOOL IN THE UNITED STATES.

⁂

Copyright ©1973 by Nicholas Zook
Library of Congress Catalog Card Number 72-92469
International Standard Book Number 0-8271-7251-6
(paper edition ISBN 0-8271-7252-4)
All rights reserved
Designed by Patricia Maka
Composed by Atlantic Typographers
Printed by The Nimrod Press

TABLE OF CONTENTS

CHAPTER 1
NEW ENGLAND
GARDENS

To explore New England's more than one hundred fifty gardens open to the public is many things.

It is to delve into the nature of earlier American life through an examination of period gardens. You will see how the garden areas were integrated with both the simplest of homes and the most stately, and you will encounter many old-fashioned flowers, no longer grown commercially.

It is to admire the infinite variety in the design of gardens, each one an individual creation. For no two gardens are alike. Even those which follow a simple and basic geometric pattern differ in the manner in which plant materials are grouped for effect.

It is to find the unexpected retreat in the heart of a bustling city or the pastoral charm of an old-fashioned garden in a scenic, rural setting.

Gardens were an immediate necessity to the Pilgrims who landed on the shores of Plymouth, Massachusetts, in 1620. They furnished food for sustenance in plots, away from the house, which the menfolk cleared of timber and stone. They furnished herbs for medicinal and household purposes in kitchen gardens planted and nurtured by women in the household. And, soon after the herbs were planted, the kitchen gardens were bright with flowers simply for their beauty.

The nature of the soil and climate in New England was such that the Reverend Francis Higginson, writing of a visit to Salem in 1629, said:

Divers excellent pot-herbs grow abundantly among the Grasse, as Strawberrie leaves in all places of the countrey, and plenty of Strawberries in their time, and Penny royall, Winter Savorie, Brooklime, liverwort, Carwell and Watercresse, also Leakes and onions are ordinarie, and divers Physicall Herbes.

Here also are abundance of other sweet Herbes delightful to the smell, whose names we know not, &c. and Plentie of single Damaske Roses verie sweet; and two kinds of Herbes that bear two kinds of Flowers verie sweet, which they say, are as good to make Cordage or Cloath as any Hempe or Flax we have.*

❖❖❖

The first kitchen gardens were shapeless and functional. They were borders, squares or rectangles of tilled earth, close by the kitchen door. But, with time, they were shaped and planted with an eye to pleasing the senses of sight and scent. Beds were raised and edged, walks were made of stone or pebbles, and fences added definition.

The gardens became a happy marriage between plant varieties native to America and those long-known in the Old World. England's roses, tulips and herbs shared beds with American varieties of the iris, lily and violet.

With increasing prosperity, the gardens of New England took on new dimensions. They indeed became pleasure gardens with wide walks, hedges of privet, or of sweetbrier and whitethorn, with perhaps a corner arbor for relaxation.

In the nineteenth century, the landscape architects came into their own, many of them putting to their own uses the formal designs of the estate gardens of Europe. They imported or had sculpted such accessories as Roman and Grecian columns and statuary to give their gardens added interest. They shaped immense formal beds in more immense sweeps of lawn.

One of the finest examples of this later period is the garden of The Elms, the former Edward J. Berwind mansion, now a property of the Preservation Society of Newport County, Newport, Rhode Island.

The Elms, a summer villa completed in 1901 during Newport's Age of Elegance, was designed by the Philadelphia architect, Horace Trumbauer, in the style of eighteenth century France. While the main house and furnishings cost more than $709,000, the cost of boundary walls and improvement of grounds was $272,307, each a tidy sum in that or any other era.

The magnificent garden, tended in its heyday by as many as twelve gardeners, must be seen in context with the magnificent mansion, a two-story marble edifice with oversize French windows. The visitor passes clipped beeches, maples, lindens and gingkos along the entrance drive and massed rhododendrons along the front of the villa.

Skirting the house, he will find at the rear a raised terrace overlooking broad lawns and gardens. In the distance are two marble teahouses or gazebos.

While large urns and statuary punctuate the terrace, a bronze group, the Madness of Athamas, dominates it. A path leads to a bronze fountain on which Hercules is depicted in the act of slaying the Hydra. Niches are clipped into a thick hedge and the spaces created are

* "New England's Plantation, or a Short and True Description of the Commodities and Discommodities of That Countrye, Written by a reverend Divine now there resident," published in England, 1630.

occupied by marble busts on high pedestals.

Beyond the lawn, which could easily accommodate several football fields, is the sunken garden, a prize package indeed. The lawn ends at a terrace area, which overlooks the garden.

The garden is entered by staircases at either the north or the south teahouse. Within the enclosure, shaped privets stand like sentinels about two large flower beds. Double rings of boxwood hedges encircle others. The flowers, both annuals or perennials, change with the season.

Here again statuary plays an important part in overall effect. An Italian wellhead with a frieze of dancing cherubs and a goat embellishes the center of the garden. On one side, there is a fountain with a sculpture grouping of four boys with their feet resting on the heads of dolphins. A second fountain has three dolphin heads spewing water into a rectangular pool.

It is indeed a magnificent garden of an age of elegance.

❈❈❈

I began my exploration of New England gardens by soliciting lists from state agencies and horticultural societies. I also contacted major garden clubs. The results were spotty. I learned no complete or accurate listing existed for any of the states.

I found on lists some gardens which no longer existed. Their creators had died, or abandoned their gardens, or sold their property. Housing subdivisions now sprawled in some areas where open gardens once flourished. A lack of funds for maintenance had closed other gardens. One inquiry to a house museum brought the reply, "No longer a garden because no gardener."

Some gardens that once delighted thousands of visitors were no longer open to the public. In one case, the garden was open only to residents of the town in which it was located. The altered climate of American life was such that their owners or caretakers were fearful of vandals and intruders. They were also concerned about careless littering.

But I also learned many new gardens had been planted for public enjoyment, once more swelling the total. Responsible for many of these gardens were garden clubs, today more active in the field of civic beautification than ever before.

Many clubs are landscaping and maintaining plantings around municipal buildings and restoring gardens at house museums. They are battling pollution and teaching garden therapy at rehabilitation centers.

The achievements of garden clubs in the Greater Boston area alone have been impressive in recent years.

The Reading Garden Club planted small gardens in the downtown area, the Stoneham Garden Club maintains the grounds of the Stoneham Library, the Belmont Garden Club created mini-parks for the elderly in the heart of the town.

The Cambridge Plant and Garden Club maintains the gardens at the historic *Longfellow House* (1759) on Brattle Street in Cambridge. The Arlington Garden Club significantly reduced pollution in a brook. The Green Thumb Club planted a garden for the aged in Medford.

In Chelmsford, near the New Hampshire border, five garden clubs joined forces to renovate the *Barrett-Byam Homestead Museum*, a newly acquired property of the Chelmsford Historical Society.

The Chelmsford Garden Club planted the front of the house. The Open Gate Garden Club of Chelmsford completed the right side of the house which was divided into three sections, the first of which is a double-tiered and somewhat formal garden. The Laurel Garden Club took care of the right side of the upper driveway and an area along a stone wall. The Buttonwood Garden Club planted a kitchen herb garden. And the Golden Chain Garden Club took care of an area beneath a curved stone wall.

❋

A most delightful garden in Stockbridge, Massachusetts, could not have survived without the continuing support of garden clubs. This is the *Berkshire Garden Center*, eight nicely land-scaped acres with such diverse areas as a rose garden, herb garden, daffodil bank, lily pond and greenhouse.

The center, a nonprofit corporation chartered to gather and disseminate "among its members and the public information and knowledge of plant life and gardening," had an accidental beginning.

The gently sloping land it occupies was under consideration as a site for a new gasoline station in 1934. The prospect of such a blemish on the rural landscape prompted a nearby resident, Mrs. Bernhard Hoffman of Stockbridge and Santa Barbara, California, to buy the property.

She interested the Lenox Garden Club in helping establish a garden center on the site. Within weeks, thirty-five representatives of various parts of Berkshire County met to organize the center and later to appoint a horticul-tural director. Today, representatives of twenty-nine garden clubs, some as distant as Albany, New York, serve as trustees.

From the beginning, garden clubs played a significant role in shaping the course of the center. A dwarf apple orchard was given to the center by the Great Barrington Garden Club. The Williamstown Garden Club contributed a shade area. The Lenox Garden Club donated the *Beatrice Procter Memorial Garden* "to continue the good taste in harmonious design and color" of one of the center's most enthusiastic supporters.

Today the center has twenty-eight distinct areas, its diversity making it in effect a botanical garden. A dominant feature is a terraced herb garden with an arbor entrance. At the car entrance along Route 102, two parallel beds border the driveway with seasonal displays such as daffodils, pansies, geraniums and chrysanthemums. Hybrid teas, floribundas and miniatures are mixed in the rose garden. Tuberous begonias are on exhibition in the summer in the lath house. There is a dwarf conifer collection in one area, and a juniper and conifer planting in another.

The visitor may expect to see flowers from late April to mid-October. He may also visit the greenhouses in winter months to inspect a wide range of plants and flowers.

Garden clubs aid the resident horticulturist, C. Roy Boutard, in planning and supporting special events throughout the year.

A major event for more than thirty-five years has been a harvest festival, held in early October as a means of raising funds for the center. Garden club members and friends donate

9

costume jewelry, books, toys and antiques for the various booths.

A major contributing group has been the center's Herb Associates. In one recent year alone, the associates worked through the summer months to make 175 catnip mice, 480 jars of herb mustard, and 447 bags for lavender and moth-proof mix, all from the center's herb garden.

They also made 1263 jars of various jellies and filled 7177 assorted bags, bottles and jars with herb products which were placed on sale at the Herb House. From this total effort, the center realized more than $2800.

While the Berkshire Garden Center places much emphasis on lectures and symposiums for adults, it has not ignored the young. Its youth center has introduced thousands of youngsters from Berkshire County school systems to the wonders of nature.

Classes come to see flowers from different parts of the world and to study the life cycle of a tree, from germination on. They see plants that like winter and those that can't tolerate it.

In one of the center's periodic publications, "Cuttings," summer 1971, Boutard wrote,

To see, feel, taste and hear — those are the experiences the Garden Center has to offer the many grade school classes.

To see may be the first experience as young people enter the Procter Garden. Lavender lilacs, yellow doronicum, purple violas, bluebells, trillium, and forget-me-nots all appeal quickly to the eyes, but the scent of the lilacs and the pink azaleas is quickly noticed. Seed heads of Anemone pulsatilla (or pasque flower) are not prickly as suspected, but soft and gentle.

As we go out through the back of the garden, the veins of the many different hosta leaves are firm to the touch, and as we look up at the size of the big maples, the height seems enormous. Ask the students what they enjoy with their pancakes and they can almost taste the sweetness of maple syrup as we look at the old spigot left in the tree from the past year's maple syrup sap season. The patch of poison ivy on an old ash tree can cause the correct amount of dread and excitement.

This is the introduction to gardens that the center has to offer.

❋

To explore New England gardens is to meet enthusiasts for whom nothing is more exciting or satisfying than making the good earth yield a bounty of bloom.

One such enthusiast is William C. Rae, who has turned the *Edgewood Gardens'* campus of American International College in Springfield, Massachusetts, into thirty-six acres of color during the warm weather months.

Thousands of sightseers each year seek out the campus, located in a model cities area, to admire the fifty-two huge beds of flowers, set off by trim lawns. The biggest attraction is a giant bed in which the letters, AIC, formed with yellow coleus, stand out against a background of irisene.

The blooming pattern of more than twenty-six thousand plants, set in beds with diamond, circle and half arch shapes, is such that there is full bloom throughout most of the summer. All plants are annuals, and the great majority are grown from seeds and cuttings.

These huge gardens had a small beginning. Rae, a native of Scotland, came to Springfield in 1928 to work in four large greenhouses which were a part of the former Reed Estate. The greenhouses, each 40 feet wide by 150 feet long, were planted to yield cut flowers for commercial purposes.

A year later they were leased to Springfield Florist Supply which hired Rae to run them. The enterprise operated until 1950 when American International College bought the estate. Rae was given a three-year lease to operate the greenhouses on the condition that he care for the college grounds at the same time. When the lease expired, the college found an urgent need for the land and eliminated the greenhouses. Rae, however, stayed on as grounds supervisor.

"In the following year," Rae explained, "I planted hedgerows along some paths on campus and a few beds of annuals. I made additional beds in succeeding years. There were two long beds with red geraniums bordered with yellow coleus. Two others with marigolds were filled with plants which grew to graduated heights. And finally I formed the bed, on a slope in front of the gymnasium, with the AIC sign. That drew a lot of attention, and from that point on there were streams of visitors on campus during the summer months."

Rae chooses to plant with annuals because perennials have a shorter season. The annuals provide blossoms from May to frost and are at their height in September, when the students return for the fall semester.

He has a small greenhouse and a large ground area with cold frames in which he propagates his seeds and cuttings. He will start from seeds, like those of begonias, during the second week of February and will sow every other week to late March. He will take cuttings of geraniums in October and root them in sand. They will go from sand to pots for the winter, yielding as many as thirty-two hundred geraniums. He will finish his seeding with marigolds which grow quickly. The plants go from greenhouse to cold frame to flower beds.

He begins setting out plants in beds during early April, first putting out petunias and sweet alyssum. Other species are set in place at the appropriate time until the yellow coleus is planted in early June.

Rae's is an organic garden. He tills leaves and flowers into the beds when the growing season is over. He adds some lime and dried fertilizer in the spring.

※※※

To explore New England's open gardens is to gain an insight into the lives of the famous, those distinguished men and women who balanced achievement in the world with a close communion with nature through their gardens.

Such a one was Daniel Chester French, the sculptor whose noted works include the Minute Man statue which fronts the North Bridge in Concord, Massachusetts, the seated Lincoln in the Lincoln Memorial in Washington, D.C., and George Washington, with sword held high, in Paris.

French and his wife made New York City their home when they embarked on a carriage trip through the Housatonic River Valley in 1896. They were smitten with the Berkshire Hills and immediately bought the 150-acre Marshall Warner farm in Stockbridge, Massachusetts.

THE HISTORIC STUDIO OF DANIEL CHESTER FRENCH IN STOCKBRIDGE, MASSACHUSETTS

The farm, with a view of the Housatonic River and Monument Mountain, was transformed into a summer estate which included an elaborate studio and gardens.

French was to say later, "I live here six months of the year — in heaven. The other six months I live, well — in New York."

French named his estate *Chesterwood*. Today, a large portion of that estate — the art studio, a nearby barn gallery, the gardens and wood-land nature trails — is open to the public. It was donated to the National Trust for Historic Preservation in 1969 by Mrs. Margaret French Cresson in memory of her father. The property is a National Historic Landmark and a Massachusetts Historic Landmark.

Many come to Chesterwood to see the studio, a thirty-foot stucco and frame cube, containing models and works completed by French and works in progress at his death in 1931. There is also a small room for casting models and a reception room where French entertained guests.

Many come to see the Barn Gallery with its display of French works, its exhibits related to his early life, and its portraits and sculptures of French family members.

But all who come to see these linger to savor the gardens and the series of nature trails beyond them.

French took a personal interest not only in the design of the garden but also in the work that went into its maintenance. He was not loathe to weed and prune and to bury his fingers in the rich earth.

French set the studio area off from the summer residence by erecting a brick wall close by the studio and planting a lilac hedge for some distance farther along.

The main garden is located on a raised terrace immediately in front of the studio. Between the studio entrance and steps leading onto the terrace is a marble fountain designed by Henry Bacon, the architect, and embellished by French. It is just beyond this fountain on the lip of the terrace that Isadora Duncan is reputed to have danced during a visit.

French liked terminal points and both garden and nature trails have them. A peony path on the terrace continues to a graceful wrought iron archway. A portion of lawn stretches to an arbor. A flower border extends along the side of the terrace retaining wall and ends at two marble columns which flank the entranceway to the nature trails.

Pieces of statuary by French and others dot the nature trails French mapped out and loved to walk. There are also occasional benches in the hemlock glade with its outcroppings of rock and its ground covers of myrtle and pachysandra. French particularly loved one trail, leading to an overlook with a distant view of valleys and hills.

The nature trails that French created are but a few of the many scattered throughout New England. While the main intent of this book is to provide a broad picture of open gardens, the picture would not be complete without some emphasis on nature trails and sanctuaries.

Many are rich in wildflower areas and gardens, and some have within their confines formal plantings, such as a herb garden.

❊

One such area with great appeal to children is the *Sharon Audubon Center* in Sharon, Connecticut, maintained by the Audubon Society.

The 526-acre wildlife sanctuary with its variety of habitats was established in 1961 through the generosity of Mr. and Mrs. Clement Ford. It has nine miles of trails and two lakes with abundant wildlife.

Within the sanctuary is a herb garden which is maintained by the Millbrook Garden Club. The garden is a large rectangular area with a sundial in its center. It has broad walks and brick-lined beds with scores of species of annual and perennial herbs.

The center is a "community center" where people of all ages may take part in various programs. There are guided tours, bird walks, adult natural history workshops, and a summer program for young people.

School and youth groups during a visit are given a brochure, prepared by Carolyn MacNeil, a teacher at the center. It is admirably written and illustrated to stimulate interest.

It begins, "Here is an invitation to an adventure. The program is outside. You are a participant. Your role is one of enjoyment, observation and discovery by using your senses. We hope your adventure will help you gain some understanding of the interrelatedness of the environment."

The pamphlet, printed on recycled, reclaimed waste paper, touches on each of twenty-three distinct areas along the marked trail. Here are some of the stops along the way.

Cross spillway on stepping stones.

3. A good place for THINKING. *Stop a while and notice how many kinds of habitats there are in your view. Look to the sky. Clouds today? Designs in the clouds?*

4. The FOREST — *an immediate difference in light, wind and moisture. Can you feel it? Where differences meet,* CHANGES *occur. What are the dominant trees?*

5. This natural bed of ferns contains a number of species. Ferns are green plants which have roots, stems, and leaves, but no flowers. They reproduce by spores which are on the underside of a frond or on a separate spike. Have you seen ferns unfolding from their "fiddlehead" in Spring?

With such a guide as this, what child could fail to become intrigued with nature's own garden?

❦

To explore New England is to find sheltered garden retreats in busy places. Such a one in the heart of Salem, Massachusetts, is that on the grounds of *The First Church, Salem,* formerly the First Congregational Society (Unitarian), gathered in 1629.

The gothic-style church is located close by the historic Ropes Mansion and the Witch House, both visited by thousands of tourists during the warm weather months. The garden, enclosed on three sides by high fences, is not visible from the road.

A visitor must enter the grounds and walk along the side of the church to find the gate in the low, wrought-iron fence which leads into the garden.

The garden, now in its fourth century, dates from 1642 when it was owned by the Corwins, who built the Witch House. It was bought in 1761 by Dr. Ebenezer Putnam "for a garden for my mansion" [now the Red Cross House]. It was purchased by The First Church in 1948 and, since 1955, has been transformed into a church garden through the labor of volunteers.

The garden retains many of the best features of each century, horticulturally, architecturally and spiritually. Many are original, some restored. That objective has taken volunteers to the history of the church and the city, to town records and those of the Essex Institute in Salem.

The garden is perhaps forty feet square with wrought iron and concrete benches placed discreetly in various corners. Borders along the fence follow flowing curves. Ancient wisteria is espaliered along one fence and covers a memorial arbor. The central lawn area is shaded by several varieties of low-growing trees.

There are Georgian urns here and there and, to one side, a fountain. Spots of color are provided by an arbor of roses and, in season, by tulips, rhododendrons, tall lilacs, and chrysanthemums. It is a most restful garden.

A completely different type of garden area in Massachusetts can be explored by bicycle. That vehicle will take you along the bicycle trail through the heart of the forty-four hundred acre former *Province Lands State Reservation*, now part of the Cape Cod National Seashore. The eight-mile paved trail wanders through forests, beside ponds and bogs, and over some of the most spectacular dunes along the Atlantic coast.

The trail in Provincetown, at the tip of the cape, penetrates a densely wooded area where swamp azalea, sweet pepperbush, blueberry and fetterbush grow on the borders of ponds and marshes. Here and there are patches of wintergreen or lady's-slippers and bright, showy goldenrod.

Along sand dunes you will find beach grass intermingling with beach pea, seaside goldenrod, dusty miller and salt spray roses. There are stands of red maple, black oak, sassafras and birch. In some areas there is an assortment of native pitch pine mixed with Scotch, Mugo and Austrian pine, all exotics planted in an effort to arrest the drifting sand dunes.

Portions of this historic area were set aside as early as 1670 by the "Plimoth Colony" in pioneering conservation action.

※※※

There are, of course, certain times of the year when the visitor may not only inspect open gardens but may also take part in garden oriented events.

An example is the *Dogwood Festival*, held for two weeks in early May in the village of Greenfield Hill in the town of Fairfield, Connecticut. The festival, an institution for more than thirty-five years, attracts busloads of visitors from as many as thirty-five states.

The whites and pinks and radiant reds of dogwood flower early in May in Connecticut. They may be found in profusion along the parkways of Fairfield County, clustered by the roadway and sparkling from the deeper woods beyond.

The village of Greenfield Hill has more than thirty thousand dogwood trees, large numbers of them clustered about the Greenfield Hill Congregational Church and its environs, which have been declared a National Historic Site.

Capitalizing on that fact, the Women's Guild of the church began sponsoring a two-week dogwood festival in 1936. The festival features a variety of typical "New England church fair" attractions.

A tent on the church lawn has a variety of hand-crafted articles for sale. Another has tables laden with homemade foods. Flower stalls are sales points for house plants, annuals, perennials and herbs.

Two separate house and garden tours are arranged with the cooperation of various area organizations. Throughout the festival, ladies of the church provide a "sit down" luncheon in the white colonial edifice. They also offer picnic-style fixings for those who wish to enjoy their meal among the dogwood groves.

But the dogwoods remain the prime attraction and visitors, starting from the church, may wander for hours among the blossoms without repeating a single view or vista.

※※※

It is the unexpected find that delights one on a garden motor tour. During one garden safari day, I concentrated on the Maine towns of Wiscasset, Rockport and Camden, all along the coast north of Portland.

Wiscasset is one of the most charming and scenic towns in New England. Shipowners and sea captains had built large mansions there during the days of clipper ships. The graceful houses, most of them white, still stand solidly along tree-lined streets, now mainly the homes of writers and artists.

I had come to inspect the garden of the *Nickels-Sortwell House* at Main and Federal streets. The federal mansion, built in 1807, has long been famed for its imposing façade and its period furniture and furnishings.

The garden was not pretentious. Borders at the side of the house consisted largely of day lilies and tall lilacs. Granite steps led to a rear lawn, bordered by perennial beds.

What was more impressive was a sunken garden I chanced upon directly across the street. The garden has been created in what had been the cellar of a large house on Main Street. Granite steps lead from sidewalk to garden.

A SUNKEN GARDEN IN WISCASSET, MAINE

Within the stone foundation walls, a town committee had planted and maintains annuals and perennials in flower borders and in four beds. Brick walks and two benches complete the charming picture. Adjacent to the sunken garden at street level is a broad lawn with tall white birch trees for shade.

Large and impressive houses line the streets of somnolent Rockport, farther north on Route 1. Its elevated location provides occasional glimpses of the sea as you drive through the town. In the center, the town has created a small park with lawns and benches. From this hillside vantage point, a visitor may watch boats at anchor in the bay or sailing the ocean waters.

What is surprising in this town of fewer than two thousand residents is the existence of a *children's chapel* with immaculate grounds and gardens.

The chapel, conceived and built for public use more than twenty years ago by Mrs. Helene Bok, a Rockport resident, stands on a promontory with a view of the sea. It is a simple wood structure with a cathedral ceiling. It is completely open to the elements at front and back and partially open at both sides. The interior is equipped with benches, and an altar on a stone floor.

Stairs on both sides of the building go down to several garden areas. A circular garden, at the time of my visit, was rich with columbines, snapdragons and zinnias. A variety of annuals and perennials gave color to a rectangular garden between the two stairways.

Even more appropriate to the chapel theme was a herb garden, enclosed by stone walls.

Here, in raised beds separated by stone paths, were herbs mentioned in the Bible.

The neighboring town of Camden is another attractive coastal resort town. Its Town Landing is home for a number of old-time schooners, available for six-day cruises along the coast of Maine. Many of its impressive homes are open during one day in July when the Camden Garden Club sponsors a tour of homes and gardens.

While these gardens are open one day a year, the gardens which are a part of the *Bok Amphitheater* are open year around. Benefactor for the unusual amphitheater was Mrs. Bok, who created the children's chapel.

When the town library was being built on its hillside site, Mrs. Bok arranged to have the amphitheater built behind it, partly on library grounds and partly in a shore front park.

The amphitheater, completed in 1931, is a horseshoe-shaped expanse of lawn, perhaps 150 by 200 feet, encircled by a series of steps and tiers, reminiscent of ancient Roman amphitheaters. It is capable of seating three thousand persons at such events as high school graduations, plays and concerts.

Beyond the tiered seats are trees, shrubs, ferns and other plants, all native to Maine and all gathered from spots within ten miles of Camden. The seats, facing the open mouth of the horseshoe, command an impressive view of boats on Penobscot Bay.

These, then, are some of the gardens you may see in New England.

CHAPTER 2
ARBORETUMS
AND BOTANICAL
GARDENS

The arboretums of the world are living museums of woody plants, while the botanical gardens are broader in scope. They are not only devoted to shrubs and trees but they also embrace herbaceous plants and, generally, include a conservatory.

The general purpose of both is the advancement and the spread of plant knowledge. It is to these establishments that the gardener may come to view new and old plant varieties which may enhance his own garden. It is also there that the layman may stroll in a park setting, a tranquil retreat from city life.

Of all planned gardens in New England, the arboretums and botanical gardens have the greatest variety of plant materials.

Some are comparatively small in size. The *Fay Hyland Botanical Plantation* at the University of Maine at Orono, Maine, for example, is about three acres. It is essentially a collection of native trees and shrubs but several exotics have been included, especially conifers. The first three plantings were made in conjunction with Maine Day of 1935. At present, more than three hundred species of trees and shrubs have been introduced, along with species of ferns and flowering plants.

***

Others range in size up to the three hundred fifty acre arboretum and botanic garden at *Connecticut College* in New London, Connecticut. The arboretum, located immediately adjacent to the college campus, was established in 1931 and is administered by the college's Botany Department.

Some arboretums are limited in scope. An example is the *Jesse Helper Arboretum* at the

THE CONNECTICUT ARBORETUM, ADJACENT TO CONNECTICUT COLLEGE IN NEW LONDON

University of New Hampshire in Durham. It consists of more than two hundred large lilacs of several species. It is located on the hillside below the administration building and is unique in that it can be viewed from both ground and elevated levels.

Some of the botanical gardens range far in the horticultural field.

An example is the *Alexandra Botanic Garden* and the *Hunnewell Arboretum*, a part of Wellesley College in Wellesley, Massachusetts. Its twenty-one acres, set aside in 1923, have a broad collection of ornamental trees and shrubs, some natural woodlands, two ponds, and an artificial brook so well laid out that it has become naturalized.

Its *Margaret C. Ferguson Greenhouses*, open

19

to the public throughout the year, contain the only large collection of tropical plants in the area.

✻✻✻

Another example is the *Botanic Garden of Smith College* in Northampton, Massachusetts. A large portion of the three-hundred acre campus is designated as an arboretum. Sections here are devoted to trees and shrubs in the different plant families.

In one area, a garden for the use of the Department of Biological Sciences consists of a series of beds, each with a plant family represented in it. This is for the study of taxonomy.

A formal garden behind one of the dormitories has a small rose collection and formal beds of annuals. Its main function is ornamental.

And a greenhouse on campus is reputed to house the largest greenhouse plant collection in New England. The collection includes tropical, succulent, warm temperate, and purely ornamental plants.

✻✻✻

Others are among the most extensive gardens in terms of species and varieties. The *Arnold Arboretum* in the Jamaica Plain section of Boston, Massachusetts, long a leader in searching out new shrubs and tree varieties throughout the world, has more than six thousand varieties of plants available for your inspection.

Oldest of New England arboretums is the Arnold Arboretum, which celebrated its centennial in 1972. It lays claim to being the first botanic garden in America devoted exclusively to the study and growing of woody plants.

The arboretum holds a distinguished place in the annals of American gardening. It intro-

duced countless shrubs and trees, including many now common ornamentals, to gardeners in the United States.

It developed the Arnold crab apple from a chance seedling. During the first decades of this century, its plant collectors brought back hundreds of new plants from the Orient. Among these are the Japanese barberry, Wilson barberry, scores of varieties of rhododendrons, privet honeysuckle, paperbark maple, and the dove tree.

The arboretum, financed completely by endowments and private donations, is administered by Harvard University with the cooperation of the Boston Department of Parks and Recreation. That union of school and city was the product of necessity in the early years of the arboretum.

Here is how it came about.

James Arnold, a wealthy New Bedford shipping merchant, died on December 3, 1869, leaving an endowment of $103,847 to be used for the promotion of agricultural or horticultural improvement.

His trustees, George B. Emerson, John James Dixwell and Francis E. Parker, all of Boston, decided a tree trial garden would suit the purpose. They approached Harvard University with a proposal that the university use the endowment to establish such a garden.

The President and Fellows of Harvard College signed an agreement on March 29, 1872, to do so. Harvard, coincidentally, had been given land in what was then West Roxbury by Benjamin Bussey, a Boston merchant, for the benefit of agricultural education.

The university combined the Arnold endow-

IRISES IN BLOOM AT THE ARNOLD ARBORETUM, BOSTON

ment with one hundred twenty-five acres of the Bussey land to form the Arnold Arboretum.

First director of the arboretum and one who held that post until his death in 1927 was Charles Sprague Sargent. He was a happy choice. Sargent was a dedicated and innovative director who did big things on a tiny budget.

He persuaded Frederick Law Olmsted, the famous landscape architect, to draw up an overall plan for the arboretum grounds. Olmsted took advantage of the terrain to lay out roads and paths which curved up and down hills to provide new vistas at each turn. Sargent's budget was not enough, however, to implement the plan.

That impasse was hurdled after long negotiations through an agreement between Harvard and the City of Boston. Harvard donated the land to the city, formally making the tract a part of the city system of parks. The city fenced in the land, built walks and roads, and agreed to provide police patrols.

The city in turn leased back the land to Harvard for one thousand years at a token fee with the understanding that Harvard would maintain the arboretum as a park.

Today, more than half a million persons a year visit the park. From early April when the early forsythias, daphne, and Cornelian cherry bloom to September when the native clematis and in October when Franklinia (native witch-hazel) is in flower, the visitors may revel in splashes of color.

At the same time, the arboretum staff continues its task of identifying, studying and propagating plants. It also receives and sends plants and seeds from and to every part of the globe and keeps in touch with plant students the world over.

Sargent's immediate goal was to grow specimens of every woody plant that could survive in the Boston climate. To this end, he and staff members combed the world for new woody plants, sending seeds and cuttings back to America.

In 1906, he hired Ernest Henry Wilson, an Englishman who was to become one of the great collectors of plants in modern times. Wilson mounted expedition after expedition to the Orient during the next twenty-four years, bringing back thousands of plants.

His efforts were such that, on two typical trips, he provided the arboretum with seeds, cuttings or plants of 1193 species and varieties. The arboretum propagated 918 of these and came up with four new genera, 521 new species and 356 new varieties.

Research and field trips continue to be very much a part of the arboretum under the present director, Richard A. Howard. Staff members travel the world still to study such fields as the flora of China or gentians in the tropics.

The arboretum through the years has given away literally millions of plants. It has done this, in part, to make plants available to the average gardener. It has also done this to place plants in different temperature zones to determine their hardiness and their reaction to such factors as sandy soil and seacoast locations.

Its greenhouses continue to experiment with methods of propagation. Since some seeds keep their dormancy for a long time, methods must be devised to hasten their germination. Some are refrigerated to simulate winter's cold, a means of hastening the time clock for germination. Other seeds are treated with concentrated sulphuric acid or perforated with a three-cornered file to quicken the sprouting process.

There are perhaps one hundred ninety arboretums or botanical gardens in the United States. Over the years, the Arnold Arboretum has remained one of a handful with major resources for research.

It has also grown in size and scope. The original 125 acres in Jamaica Plain is now 265 acres. In addition, the arboretum occupies two other sites.

A portion of the herbarium and library is in Cambridge, at Harvard University. The herbarium is not a display collection, but provides plant specimens for study by students.

The other location is the Case Estates in Weston, Massachusetts, a 112-acre tract thirteen miles away. The Weston site is basically a nursery and teaching area for the arboretum.

※

The *Case Estates* were a gift, along with an endowment, to the arboretum from the late Misses Marian Roby Case and Louisa Case. The endowment provides funds for many horticultural experiments, work in test gardens, display areas, and ornamental shrub nurseries.

The existence of the Case Estates in its present form is a tribute to Marian Roby Case (1864–1944), a remarkable woman and horticulturist.

On land she inherited and increased through purchase Miss Case, for thirty-three years until her death, conducted a school of agriculture and gardening during summer months for children of Weston and surrounding towns.

She employed up to twenty boys each summer to work Hillcrest Farm, later known as *Hillcrest Gardens*, and to attend classes on botany, agriculture and farming. She also provided them uniforms and a clubhouse.

Hillcrest was a truck farm, but the income from the produce never equaled the cost of the school and Miss Case's many horticultural philanthropies. Hillcrest Gardens used the latest methods of cultivation and followed closely the agricultural developments of the day.

Miss Case inaugurated an annual series of lectures, held generally on Wednesday afternoons, dealing with some facet of nature or agriculture. During a period of thirty years, one hundred fifteen men, including college presidents, outstanding scientists and former Hillcrest boys, appeared on the lecture program.

During winter travels, Miss Case established contacts in Italy, Sicily, Greece and Egypt, where she collected seeds and also had seeds of potentially useful ornamentals sent to Weston for trial. Hillcrest Gardens became the first spot

EXPERIMENTAL FLOWER BEDS AT THE CASE ESTATE, WESTON, MASSACHUSETTS

in New England to try many South African herbaceous plants.

At her death, she deeded her land to Harvard University, just as her sister, Louisa Case, had given it some fifty-nine acres of adjoining Case property, including her residence, as a memorial to her father, James B. Case.

The Case Estates have about twenty-five hundred species and varieties of plants being grown in nurseries. Some are replacements for old plants in the arboretum, and some are introductions new to America.

Since the arboretum in Jamaica Plain is limited in space, it places many of the plants it can't exhibit in nursery areas at Weston. The arboretum has five hundred different varieties of lilacs, for example. It has retained three hundred of them in Jamaica Plain and maintains the balance at Weston.

Both the arboretum and the Case Estates have self-guiding tours.

The one at the arboretum will take you through areas with concentrations of such plants as mock orange, azaleas which bloom in sequence, and espaliered shrubs. It will also take you by stands of larches, beeches, crab apples, and Asiatic oaks, to mention only a few.

The tour at the Case Estates will take you to twenty-seven distinct areas. These include a specimen tree area, a rhododendron collection, and a hosta display collection.

Daffodil trial plots are maintained in co-operation with the American Daffodil Society. Hemerocallis display plots were donated by the American Hemerocallis Society.

There is also a low maintenance perennial garden where dwarf shrubs, mulched with pine needles to reduce labor, grow. Old-fashioned bulb varieties appear in spring. The swamp area has cowslips, double cardamine, and forget-me-nots, followed by blue and yellow swamp iris.

❄❄

More recent in origin is the *Connecticut Arboretum*, established in 1931 and administered by the Botany Department at Connecticut College in New London, Connecticut.

Its director, William A. Niering, has said, "The arboretum plays many roles. As a green belt of open space surrounding the campus, it serves as a park for the college community and the residents of the surrounding area.

"In our educational program it is an outdoor laboratory where students in biology, botany and zoology can study plants and animals in their natural environment. It fulfills an indispensable role in the Thames Science Center nature program and during the summer the Girl Scout Day Camp uses our facilities."

The arboretum had its beginning in 1911, at the founding of Connecticut College, when Anna Hempstead Branch, with her mother, Mary L. Bolles Branch, gave the school a sixteen-acre tract to be used as a park for the students. That property had been in the Bolles family since 1693 when Thomas Bolles bought it from a Mohegan Sachem, Owaneco, son of Uncas. Other gifts and purchases brought the arboretum to its present size of three hundred fifty acres.

The arboretum, established under the directorship of Dr. George S. Avery, Jr., divides itself quite naturally into special areas.

Its woody plant collection has about 375 species which are indigenous to the north-eastern United States, representing some 116 genera. These may be found along grassy trails where in early spring the white flash of shadbush is followed by the flowering dogwoods, hawthorns and azaleas. By mid-June the laurel path is bright with pink blossom.

Two natural areas with access trails have been permanently set aside to remain undisturbed. The Bolleswood area of one hundred sixty acres represents a ledgy, oak-hemlock forest recovering from a blowdown incurred during the 1938 hurricane. Within its confines is farm land which is now reverting to woodland, a small open bog and wooded swamps.

※※

The *Mamacoke Natural Area* of forty acres is a high, rocky promontory extending into the Thames River and connected to the mainland by a small tidal marsh.

A wildflower garden, established in memory of Mrs. Malcolm J. Edgerton by the Federated Garden Clubs of Connecticut, is located in a natural woodland setting.

On one side of the campus is an attractive display of ornamental trees and shrubs. It was originally laid out by Miss Caroline Black, former member of the Botany Department, and is named in her honor.

※※

A second arboretum in Connecticut is the *Bartlett Arboretum* in North Stamford, consisting of land formerly used by the Bartlett Tree Experts for demonstration plantings. Its sixty-two acres might have been fragmented for commercial development except for the efforts of a group of ecology-minded residents in the Stamford area.

The residents in the early 1960s formed the Bartlett Arboretum Association to generate support for the acquisition of the land by the state. Its campaign succeeded. The state bought the tract in November, 1965, under the Federal Open Spaces Program.

The tract was turned over to the University of Connecticut's College of Agriculture and Natural Resources for management and development. The Bartlett Arboretum Association continues to function as an active planning and advisory group in conjunction with representatives of the college.

The land, less than an hour from New York's Times Square, was still being farmed at the turn of the century. A large part of the arboretum is natural growth oak, maple and hickory, with a few scattered ash, birch, beech and yellow poplar.

Various walks and nature trails have been laid out and mapped. The topography is such that the tract has open field, swamp, woodland and pond habitat.

The former Bartlett residence now serves as headquarters for the arboretum. An education center there is used for group assemblies, lectures, workshops, and as a diagnostic laboratory. Funds provided by the arboretum association have been used for an extensive planting of daffodils close by the education center.

Typical of the walks is the bog walk, consisting in part of an elevated foot bridge. Trees, shrubs and various herbaceous perennials were planted here to re-create the atmosphere of a true northern bog.

Alder, shadbush, swamp azalea and blackgum flourish along the shores of a woodland pond.

The needle evergreen walk will take you by various pines, true cedars, hemlocks and many cultivars of false cypress.

A brochure at the arboretum outlines points of interest. In one area, native trees were planted in a row and are clipped annually to form a compact "poor man's hedge." Different varieties of azaleas and rhododendrons were planted to provide a home owner with a reference collection of those plants that do well in Connecticut. A grove of nut trees includes the pecan, black walnut, heartnut, the Bartlett chestnut, and the American chestnut.

The college has completed a dwarf conifer garden with more than two hundred varieties of dwarf forms of the various conifers. It set aside an area for purple foliage plants with forms of European birch, Japanese maple, beech, plum and privet. Its yellow foliage planting area has cultivars of false cypress, junipers and northern white cedar.

Inasmuch as the arboretum is located in the extreme southwestern part of Connecticut and the university is at Storrs, the college is able to evaluate the adaptability and cold hardiness qualities of plants in two quite different areas.

❋❋❋

At Storrs, the college's floriculture display and trial gardens are located on a one and a half acre grassy site. The gardens include about three hundred forty feet of perennial borders. The heart of the gardens includes two hundred different annual varieties started and grown each year. Advanced trials, new and recent varieties, All America Selections, and lesser known or unusual types are grown from seed supplied by many seed companies.

In addition to the herbaceous plants, there is a small collection of dwarf trees at Storrs, a collection of taxus, and a collection of twenty plants trained as hedges.

All plants are labeled. The best viewing period, especially for the annuals, is mid-July to mid-September.

The gardens are used for resident teaching and laboratory facilities for students in the garden flower courses during the school year. The main function of the garden in the summer is public education for visitors.

❋❋❋

An enlightened approach to campus planning was responsible for the gardens and an *arboretum* of one hundred sixty acres at *Smith College* in Northampton, Massachusetts.

L. Clarke Seelye, the first president of that college for women, was convinced the campus should be developed as a botanic garden for scientific as well as aesthetic reasons. In 1891, Olmsted, Olmsted and Eliot, a Boston firm of landscape architects, was hired to draw up plans for what was then a campus of twenty-seven acres.

With time, the campus was expanded along with the number of its gardens and greenhouses. The expansion was such that the original greenhouse of two rooms is now a complex of twelve houses, including a propagating pit and physiological laboratory. The houses cover about nine thousand square feet and contain a plant collection of more than twelve hundred labeled species and varieties.

The arboretum has some eleven hundred species and varieties of trees and shrubs. A herbaceous garden holds some six hundred labeled varieties in perennial flower beds. A rock garden contains some eight hundred labeled varieties and species of alpine, saxatile, and bulbous plants set against a background of evergreens.

All these are used for various courses in the biological sciences and for laboratory research work in plant physiology and horticulture.

In addition, two flower shows are held in the greenhouse each year. A chrysanthemum show, usually held in the first week of November, features many hybrids produced by members of past horticulture classes at Smith. There is a display of spring-flowering bulbs and plants, usually during the first week in March

Many corners of the world are represented in the various greenhouses. In the warm temperate house, there are more than one hundred species and varieties of begonia from Central and South America, the lavender-blue cape primrose from South Africa, and a collection of African violets.

The showpiece of the tropical house is a dendrobium nobile orchid which produced a hundred flowers with lavender-rimmed petals and wine-red throats. The prickly pear is represented by twenty-one species in the cactus house, and fruiting of bananas are among other plants in the palm house. Other specialized houses have species which are equally exotic.

The original plan for the campus was to set out trees and shrubs systematically by genus. The rapid expansion of enrollment, with its need for additional dormitories and classrooms, made this arrangement impractical in time.

While there are some areas devoted to such trees as red oaks, elms and honey-locusts, most areas have a mix of shrubs and trees.

You may pass here a collection of the Dexter hybrid rhododendron developed by Charles O. Dexter, and there a willow with a trunk measuring some twenty feet in circumference. A collection of the plantain lily, hosta, was a gift to the college. Appropriately, a Scotch elm was donated to the college by three Scotsmen.

There is a different and striking grouping of plantings in every part of the campus. Early spring bulbs are underplanted along a bank filled with species and varieties of azaleas, heaths, heathers, mountain laurel, and double dogwoods. Evergreen and deciduous shrubs are combined in a border by the Faculty Center. Behind Capen House a small native-plant area combines with perennial borders and arbors of roses.

College horticulturists still maintain an active program of seed exchange to assure worldwide representation of plants in the greenhouses as well as on campus. Plants in the rock garden alone represent exchanges with Paris, Stockholm, Prague, Brussels, Moscow and Tokyo.

CHAPTER 3
WILDFLOWER GARDENS AND NATURE TRAILS

The rapid disappearance of open land in a natural state has been a matter of concern for conservation forces throughout the twentieth century. Land developers have filled in bogs and swamps, diminishing areas where wildlife and wild flowers may flourish. They have bulldozed woodland where once the pink lady's-slipper and jack-in-the-pulpit blossomed.

The increasing threat to wildlife has led to the acquisition by individuals and organizations of large areas of land in New England for the purpose of conservation and preservation. These sanctuaries today embrace a varied topography, ranging from wilderness tracts to marshes and rocky promontories overlooking the sea.

One of the leaders in the battle for preservation has been *The Trustees of Reservations*, a corporation founded for conservation purposes in 1891. Its aim is to preserve for the public places of natural beauty and historic interest within the Commonwealth of Massachusetts.

The organization was the brainchild of Charles Eliot (1859–1897), son of Charles W. Eliot, then president of Harvard University. He proposed that such an organization could "hold small and well distributed parcels of land, just as the public library holds books and art museums pictures for the use and enjoyment of the public."

Today, The Trustees of Reservations are custodians for fifty-three open spaces and historic areas from the Berkshires to Cape Cod. They total more than 11,400 acres of seashore and woodlands, wetlands, marshes and wildlife areas. The land is left in its natural state to be enjoyed for its plants and flowers, its topography and wildlife.

❀❀

Another leader has been the *New England Wild Flower Society*, established in 1922 as an educational, nonprofit organization. The society is the only conservation agency in New England which is primarily concerned with the study and propagation of wild flowers and other native plants and with the preservation of their habitats.

Among the properties the society owns or controls are:

The largest stand of the great laurel in the country at Springvale, Maine.

A bog and woodland containing the northernmost stand of Atlantic white coast cedar at Bradford, New Hampshire.

A stand of luminous moss at Groton, New Hampshire.

A hardwood slope and bank along the Connecticut River, notable for its great variety of wild flowers at Plainfield, New Hampshire.

A bog and woodland filled with native orchids at Peacham, Vermont.

A wilderness tract and special sanctuary for trailing arbutus at Winchendon, Massachusetts.

A twenty-two-acre suburban sanctuary with a good collection of native plants at Weston, Massachusetts.

An extensive wild flower reservation with frontage on Merrimeeting Bay in Woolwich, Maine.

But the society's most unusual property, from the standpoint of its history, is its *Garden in the Woods* at Framingham, Massachusetts, where it maintains its headquarters and a nature center.

The garden owes its existence to the late Will C. Curtis, who gained a national reputation as a naturalistic landscape designer. Curtis stumbled on the original thirty-acre tract in 1931 and admired its mixture of stream, swamp and wooded hills. He bought the land from the Old Colony Railroad, built a house and greenhouse there, and decided to cultivate additional wildlife species.

He was joined in the project the next year by Richard H. Stiles, a horticulturist. The two men created five miles of naturalistic trails and succeeded in growing more than four thousand species and varieties of native American wild flowers.

Curtis and Stiles gave the Garden in the Woods to the New England Wild Flower Society in 1965. Their one provision was that the society raise funds as an endowment for maintenance. Within ten months the society raised $250,000 from more than one thousand individuals, foundations and garden clubs throughout the country.

The society added land to bring it up to its present forty-three acres. Within that acreage is a wide variety of habitats. There are dry, acid woodland slopes for many of the early spring flowers. A sunny bog is ideal for pitcher plants, sundews, calla lilies, and the yellow western skunk cabbage. Separate rock garden areas are devoted to New England plants, plants of the western states, and garden plants of mixed nativity.

A housing development today reaches to the entrance of the garden, testament to Curtis' foresight in buying the land for sanctuary purposes.

A visitor may park his car at the entrance and pick up a map to the self-guide trails. The trails wind among rhododendron, ferns, hemlocks and stands of white pine, hemlock and mixed hardwoods. One area is labeled a children's garden, where plants are identified and a fallen tree helps youngsters to cross a stream.

Signs identify plants and yield such nuggets of information as "Pea stone mulch helps keep weeds down, gives cool root run, conserves moisture, and keeps mud splash off plants."

The society maintains a test garden where new methods of propagation are tried out. Seed exchanges are conducted with eighty botanical institutions around the world, carrying on the work that Curtis began.

A modest bronze plaque in the ground close by the entrance of the sanctuary commemorates the name of Will C. Curtis, whose imagination and dedication made the garden possible. At his death in 1969, his ashes were scattered in the garden he loved.

※※※

Another leader in the conservation movement has been the National Audubon Society and Audubon societies within the various states. Typical of the state organizations is the Connecticut Audubon Soceity, founded in 1898, which maintains two sanctuaries with nature trails.

Birdcraft Museum and Sanctuary was started in 1914 in Fairfield. It has a museum housing the *Frank J. Novak Collection* of mounted birds and mammals. Its sanctuary area is now limited to five acres after having been gobbled up, in part, by the Connecticut Turnpike. Trees near the trails are labeled. Several of the trails lead to the main pond which features a breeding duck display.

The major property is the *Roy and Margot Larsen Aubudon Sanctuary*, also in Fairfield and headquarters for the society. The Larsen sanctuary has a land area of one hundred fifty acres which was started in 1958 when the Connecticut Turnpike condemned land at Birdcraft.

The land, the gift of the Larsens, has been intensively managed for wildlife with thousands of trees and shrubs planted, five ponds dug, and five miles of trails leading through the best areas for people to see animals.

The nature trail concept is represented on this sanctuary by a booklet, "Walk Guide," which follows numbered posts through the sanctuary. The number on a post leads one to consult the booklet for information pertaining to the area at the post.

There are forty-nine posts, and here is what you can see along the first few stops that occur on the trail.

1. Feeding thicket. *To properly set up a bird feeder, there should be plantings of shrubs for shelter. Evergreens (Norway spruce and cedar) have been planted to provide this shelter for birds. Briars grow here for ground protection.*

2. Alder swale. *The remnant stand of alder is a favorite haunt of many song birds and the preferred home of the woodcock.*

3. Marsh pond. *Financed by the Fairfield County Garden Clubs, the marsh pond was developed from a sphagnum-red maple swamp. Aquatic plants have sprung up, insects are numerous, and small fish, turtles and a variety of frogs live in the pond.*

4. Food patch and shrub nursery. *This was the only open field in the entire sanctuary but now other openings have been provided. A food patch is planted to provide seed for a variety of birds. Even deer come to the food patch.*

5. Cover change. *A clearing made by cutting swamp maples. This area will be managed to keep it in grass, weeds and medium sized shrubs.*

6. Cleared field. *Once a farm garden that had grown to solid forest, the area has been cleared of hardwoods. Natural grasses, weeds and shrubs have grown and many are food producers. Small clumps of food-bearing shrubs have been planted in the field corners, as well as a few clumps of evergreens for cover.*

There are four gardens in front of the new building which serves as the sanctuary center. These include an organic garden maintained by the Fairfield Organic Gardeners, a bog garden, fern garden, and wild flower garden.

One noteworthy feature is a walk for the blind called *Singing and Fragrance Walk for the Blind*, which was set up with funds from the Bridgeport Garden Club. The area has been extensively planted and is the sanctuary's most-used trail since most people want to experience the feeling that blind people would have in the outdoors. Many walk the trail with eyes shut.

The walkway, equipped with a guide rail of smooth logs, winds through two acres of woodland and marsh. Aromatic plants such as honeysuckle and cinnamon fern grow throughout the area, and other vegetation utilized by birds for food and nest sites have been planted near the walk. The birds congregate near the walkway, making their songs easier to hear. A small brook, which passes under bridges installed in the walkway in three places, has been channeled to create gurgling ripples.

❦

The National Audubon Society has a center in Greenwich, Connecticut, at which it operates an *Audubon Ecology Workshop* during summer months.

The center began in 1942 with a gift of 281 acres from Mrs. Eleanor Steele Reese. It reached a total acreage of 461 acres through gifts by many individuals. Among these were Mr. and Mrs. B. Tappen Fairchild, Bayard Read, Joseph Vernor Reed, Mrs. Hobart Cook, Eugene Curry, Mrs. Agnes Gayley Millikin and William F. Sanford.

❦

The various land areas are not contiguous but are within walking distance of one another. One of the areas, the *Audubon Wildflower Sanctuary* — formerly the Fairchild Connecticut Garden — consists of a varied combination of native and introduced species of plants.

Most of the plants, introduced by Benjamin Fairchild at the turn of the century, are natives of the eastern states from Maine to North Carolina. They were planted in natural settings in habitats which closely match their original environment.

The Ecology Workshop, consisting of nine week-long sessions, is designed "to provide a program in a natural setting where land and people are brought together to experience the joy and consolation which the changing landscape can provide."

The program includes field trips and the demonstration of interpretive skills and teaching methods designed for use in the outdoor classroom.

❦

The Maine Audubon Society owns seven sanctuaries and has built nature trails on three of them. The three are *Mast Landing Wildlife Sanctuary* at Freeport, the *Josephine H. Newman Sanctuary* at Georgetown, and *Appalachee Sanctuary* in Boothbay Harbor.

Mast Landing was so named because it was here that the English harvested the forests in colonial days for masts ranging from twenty-five to thirty-six inches in diameter.

The sanctuary of more than one hundred fifty acres was donated by L. M. C. Smith of Freeport. It is an oblong of land, located on a knoll, with a variety of habitats.

You will see moisture-loving plants along the short *Beaver Trail* which roughly parallels *Mill Stream*. These include skunk cabbage, jack-in-the-pulpit, marsh marigolds, meadow rue, and many ferns.

The *Woodland Trail* will take you by star flowers, wild ginger, bloodroot, bunchberry and large flowered trillium. The *Orchard Trail* has a stand of white pines and apple trees, planted more than thirty years ago.

⁂

The Massachusetts Audubon Society maintains fourteen staffed sanctuaries and thirty open spaces.

Among those that are staffed is *Laughing Brook Education Center* in Hampden, the home of beloved children's author, the late Thornton Burgess, who created the tales of Peter Rabbit and Old Mother West Wind.

Its eighty-four acres of woodland and field includes the home and barn-studio where Burgess worked. The Audubon Society has built an indoor-outdoor trail that permits the visitor to see such animals as rabbits, skunks, foxes and raccoons in their natural environment.

More than eighty volunteers assist with Mother West Wind's gift shop, public programs such as storytelling hour, and guided tours.

The Massachusetts society has its headquarters at *Drumlin Farm* in Lincoln, a legacy from Louise Ayer Hatheway. Here, it plays host to more than thirty-six thousand school children in scheduled programs every year and more than double that number of other visitors.

Tours for all ages interpret the two-hundred twenty acre farm which includes pasture, fields, woodland and ponds. The area has domestic and wild animals and birds typical to a New England farm at the turn of the century.

There are two gardens at the farm. A small, square herb garden is planted at the front of the gift shop. A demonstration garden of perhaps an acre is devoted to long rows of vegetables, each row appropriately labeled.

⁂

An unusual wildlife reservation is one located on Vinalhaven, the largest of the Fox Islands in the mouth of Penobscot Bay in Maine. The island is about seven miles long and four miles wide. Dominating the harbor is a small granite hill, now known as *Armbrust's Hill*, and it is here the reservation may be found.

William Kitteridge started the island's first commercial building stone quarry on this hill in 1840. Around 1870, the quarry was bought by James Armbrust, who carried on operations until about 1910. Ownership passed through a number of hands until it was given to the town as a wildlife reservation and educational area for the school in 1960.

32

THE MAINE AUDUBON SOCIETY ORCHARDS AT MAST LANDING IN FREEPORT

In preparation for the quarrying, most of the earth had been removed from the hill. When work stopped, shrubs and trees grew from cracks between the ledges. They shed their leaves, which rotted and mixed with granite dust to form more soil.

Moss began to flourish, followed by little potentilla tridents, then by blueberry, juniper and huckleberry. Alder, birch, mountain ash, and firs were close behind. Today a thin skin of humus supports quite tall birch and spruce and carpets of juniper hugging the rocks.

Within the twenty-five acres, wild, rangy trees probably sprang from apple cores discarded from the quarrymen's lunches. Other trees include the wild cherry and black chokeberry.

The granite hill has a number of pools, the largest about fifty feet across. Seepage from the pool has formed a small marshy area where winter berry and alder have grown tall. The

Vinalhaven Garden Club has developed this area into a wild garden.

Another pond in a nearby quarry, called the *Blacksmith*, was cleared and planted by children under the guidance of their teachers and garden club members. Plants were brought in from other parts of the island or from mainland nurseries.

The hundred-ten-foot rounded hill rises directly from Carvers Harbor, providing spectacular views of the harbor, the town, and the islands out to sea. The quarries bit into the hill on three sides, leaving cliffs thirty to forty feet high and strange ledges and castle-like formations.

Beside the main path up the hill, trails have been cut through brush to open up unexpected nooks and scenic views along the cliffs. These are called goat trails because, residents will tell you, only the agile and the foolish will use them.

Adjoining the reservation is the island's Community Medical Center, also owned by the town and landscaped by the garden club. The garden with its lily pool has a succession of blooms, mostly of wild flowers from early crocuses in May to the blue lobelia in October. There is a nearly level walk from there into the floor of the main quarry.

✳✳✳

The trails are not open to walkers at *Tupper Hill*, the *Norcross Wildlife Sanctuary* in Monson, Massachusetts. Instead, sanctuary personnel conduct motor tours in four mini-buses, pointing out various features of the sanctuary during a two-hour-long run.

The sanctuary, a three thousand acre wilderness tract, was opened to the public in 1965. It was established in 1939 by the late Arthur D. Norcross, a Monson native and head of a greeting card company. It is maintained by the Norcross Wildlife Foundation, Inc., whose purpose is the conservation of wildlife and the active practice of conservation to benefit the public.

Norcross, who died in 1969, was an ardent conservationist. He began the sanctuary in the 1930s with Tupper Hill, an estate that had been in his family for many decades. He acquired tract after tract of adjacent woodland over the years to bring it to its present size.

Norcross engineered lakes, brooks and waterfalls to blend with the rhythm of existing woods, fields and meadows. He made field trips to various parts of the country to acquire various species of trees, ferns and flowers.

A truckload of white cedar was shipped from Vermont in 1939. White dogwood and crab apple were selected from various areas and planted by a pond. From other areas he gathered flame azalea, mountain laurel, walnut trees and thorn apples. He also imported lime rocks to provide a natural habitat for ferns.

Different kinds of terrain and moisture conditions made possible a great number of naturalistic gardens for a wide variety of plants. Plants at Tupper Hill are native to the eastern seaboard from the Carolinas to Canada.

The visitor enters the gates of Tupper Hill and drives to a reception area which includes a museum and a natural history building. The museum has on its walls color photos of plants and wild flowers, each tagged to indicate what is now in bloom and what blooms have passed.

A chart lists the blooming dates as mid-April for shortia, late April for arbutus, late April and early May for trilliums, late May for dogwood and rhodora, early June for rhododendrons, mid-June for laurel, July and August for wild orchids, August for heather, and late September for gentians.

A map, given to visitors, pinpoints major

TUPPER HILL IN MONSON, MASSACHUSETTS

areas within the sanctuary. It charts the course of most of the fifty miles of roads along with the location of five pioneer home sites where layers of stone indicate house foundations.

The guide on the bus tour will point out such plants as yellow lady's-slipper, pitcher plants and swamp hyacinths. He will also draw attention to the different varieties of bird life, to turtles, and to traces of deer and beaver.

At the end of the tour, visitors are invited to wander through five areas close by the parking lot.

One is a circle garden with acid soil and partial shade, planted mostly to ground covers and ferns. A lime cobble is planted to lime-loving rock ferns.

The pine barren garden with acid soil is planted to flowers, trees and shrubs indigenous to the pine barrens of the eastern seaboard. A cedar swamp has white cedar, indigenous to the pine barrens of southern New Jersey. And a meadow garden with full sun is a natural wild flower meadow.

※※

A highly organized sanctuary is the *Blue Hills Trailside Museum* in Milton, Massachusetts. The museum is located within the six thousand acre Blue Hills Reservation, the property of the Metropolitan District Commission. It is operated by the Boston Zoological Society.

The purpose of the museum is to provide professional natural science education, using a cross-section of the natural history peculiar to the Blue Hills area. Education is provided through exhibits, lectures, trail guidance, publications and nature courses.

The museum itself, created in 1959, consists of a remodeled farmhouse with an addition which serves as an exhibition hall. Plants and trees, seen in their natural surroundings outdoors, are also exhibited indoors.

There are lifelike models of many wild flowers, mushrooms and fungi. A "planter's table" holds living wild flowers, transplanted from the reservation outside as soon as they come into bloom along the trails. There are also rocks, minerals and Indian artifacts.

The reservation has three well-marked nature trails cut through the wooded hills to provide choices for the energetic hiker or the casual stroller.

An orange trail winds through successive stages of forest growth in a leisurely fifteen-minute walk. The red trail, timed for thirty minutes, runs through an area once ravaged by forest fire and lets you see how nature heals her wounds.

The green trail, or summit trail, is a thirty-minute climb to an observation tower, built on the highest reservation hill 635 feet above sea level. Along the trails, the wild flowers you may see include the Virginia creeper, yarrow, evening primrose, lady's-slipper, and bugle weed or wild mint.

Another giant in the field of conservation is the *White Memorial Foundation*, a voluntary, nonprofit Connecticut corporation owning some four thousand acres of woodland and Bantam Lake shore front property in the towns of Litchfield and Morris.

In addition to that property, the foundation over the years acquired and deeded to the state more than five thousand acres of land for conservation and recreation purposes.

These include the *Mohawk Forest and Mountain* in Cornwall and Goshen, the greater part of *Shade Swamp Sanctuary* in Farmington, *Campbell Falls* in Norfolk and North Canaan, and *People's Forest* in Barkhamsted.

The foundation was launched by Alain C. White and his sister, May W. White, residents of Litchfield. Early in this century, they had the vision to see that Bantam Lake with its natural beauty could become an attractive recreational center or, through haphazard development, an overcrowded eyesore.

They bought large tracts of land on the shores between 1908 and 1912 and deeded them to the White Memorial Foundation, along with an endowment to help in the maintenance and development of the area.

The foundation today operates beaches and picnic areas. It owns cottages which are available for rent. It provides family campsites and has encouraged service organizations, such as the Girl Scouts, Boy Scouts, the American Youth Hostel and Young Men's Christian Association, to build camps on its grounds.

The foundation has also built and maintains some twenty-five miles of woodland roads and trails for walkers and horseback riders. A *Wild Garden*, an area of fifty acres, is maintained by the Litchfield Hills Audubon Society. A raised boardwalk around Little Pond in that area offers a close look at waterfowl and swamp growth.

These are a representative selection of nature trails for walkers and horseback riders. A *Wild Garden*, an area of fifty acres, is maintained by

CHAPTER 4
HERBS AND OLD-FASHIONED FLOWERS

The first gardens of New England were functional in design and purpose. While the men of the house planted crops in cleared fields away from the house, the women took on the responsibility of planting and maintaining their own simple kitchen gardens close by the door.

This, in some cases, consisted of an unadorned border of plants along the side of the house. In other cases, it was a more extensive plot, yet close enough so a needed herb could be fetched in seconds.

Herbs, so vital for seasoning, medicines and scores of household uses, were the mainstay of the kitchen garden. Dyeing herbs, salad herbs, vegetables and medicinal herbs coexisted in the same garden plots, with perhaps the most frequently used herbs winning a place closest by the kitchen door.

The early settlers did not neglect to bring flowers which they cherished in the Old World. They were, of course, delighted to find in the New World a profuse sprinkling of such plants, unknown to them, as the cardinal flower, pink mallow, goldenrod and aster. But these were no substitutes for the blooms they admired in the homes they left behind.

On their voyage, they brought with them the bulbs of daffodils, grape hyacinths and tulips. They also packed seeds of hollyhocks, stocks, pinks, marigolds and the dark blue English columbine. And certainly among the early arrivals were slips of English roses.

There are scores of herb gardens in New England today which are open to the public. Some follow the simple planting methods of the earliest settlers. Others, with elaborate walks and geometric designs, reflect gardens of a later period.

A RE-CREATION OF A PILGRIM KITCHEN GARDEN AT PLIMOTH PLANTATION, PLYMOUTH, MASSACHUSETTS

Also open to the public are many period gardens with old-fashioned flowers. These, filled with plant varieties no longer readily available, trace the landscaping design patterns of the eighteenth and nineteenth centuries.

❋❋

Gardens which attempt to show how the Pilgrim housewife planted for her own kitchen needs are open during the summer months at *Plimoth Plantation* in Plymouth, Massachusetts, a re-creation of the original Pilgrim village as it appeared in 1627, or seven years after they landed on the *Mayflower*.

This complex of buildings, which includes a blockhouse and simple homes with sharply pitched roofs and large fireplaces, was reproduced after research through all existing records and through archaeological research.

You will find a herb garden at each of the village houses and costumed guides or hostesses to tell you something about the more than one hundred fifty herbs used for aromatic, culinary, medicinal or dye purposes.

They will tell you that avens was put among linens to scent them and to keep moths away. The scent of horehound repelled flies and fleas. And the crushed seed pods of sweet cicely were an excellent polish for furniture.

Among culinary herbs, anise with its taste of licorice was used in cakes, candy and bread. Good King Henry was a pot herb, cooked as we cook spinach, and resembling it in taste. And the leaves of rosemary flavored fish, sauces, wine and ale.

The leaves of chicory, among the medicinal herbs, made a poultice which was applied to swellings and inflammations. The root of ele-campane, also known as sneezeweed, was boiled to produce a tonic for coughs. And a syrup made of feverfew was a cure for fevers.

Herbs play a part in the many and varied gardens at *Old Sturbridge Village* in Sturbridge, Massachusetts, a re-creation of a New England community reflecting American rural life in the period from 1790 to 1840.

The twelve-hundred acre village, which prides itself on its authenticity, consists of more than forty exhibit buildings brought together from various parts of New England. A village area with a tall-spired church and residences of different eras is centered around a typical New England green. A short distance away, the *Pliny Freeman Farm* has livestock, orchards and crops, along with related buildings such as a blacksmith shop and a grist mill. Now well on its way to completion is a manufacturing village, centered around a water-powered cotton mill.

An extensive herb garden, close by the entrance to the village, consists of a series of terraces, bounded by stone walls. Old rose varieties, such as damask and musk, used for fragrance and nosegays, flourish along the walls.

Multi-shaped beds in the upper terrace are planted largely with medicinal herbs and those used for the preservation of unrefrigerated meats. Dyeing herbs take up a great part of another bed, while seasoning herbs are sprinkled throughout.

An annual harvesting of herbs takes place at the village every fall, revealing to visitors how the Yankee housewife prepared for the winter siege by bringing in a huge variety of plants.

Medicinal and dye herbs are brought into the herb barn for drying and processing, not for the "do-it-yourself" medicines popular one hundred fifty years ago, but to make lasting winter bouquets or dried arrangements for houses on the village green.

Herb gardeners bring in basket loads of such plants as boneset, dock, cornflower, yarrow and absinthium, a variety of the artemesia family from which absinthe, the production of which has been banned since World War I, was derived. The plants are washed and hung on drying racks for a month to six weeks, then they are arranged into bouquets.

Ingredients for the potpourris are also prepared. The spiced leaves of various flowers are dried to fill small apothecary jars and then used as room scenters.

Some of these aromatic herbs include balm, basil, lavender, mint, lemon verbena, rosemary, sweet alyssum and sweet rocket.

Gardens along the walls of the older period homes are narrow borders, close by the kitchen door so the housewife might pick her mint or chives easily.

The Freeman Farm has extensive working gardens with grain, broomcorn, sunflowers and flax. A cider orchard is planted with random apple seeds, as it was in the old days.

The housewife's kitchen garden, about fifty by one hundred feet in size, has its share of herbs. It also yields most vegetables used on the family table, including peas, cabbage, onions, squash and corn.

A front dooryard garden, whose function is purely ornamental, has daylilies, iris and candytuft in narrow borders.

The most elaborate series of gardens in the village is a part of the *General Salem Towne House*, a square federal mansion erected in 1794. To one side, it has an orchard with twenty varieties of apple trees, combined with a sizable kitchen garden. Squash, turnips and other vegetables are mingled with assorted herbs in an area encircled by stone walls.

A formal garden on the opposite side of the house is embellished by a gazebo and a grape arbor. The large square garden has strips of lawn bounded by quince hedges. Brick walks surround and bisect the area, permitting a close inspection of a round center bed and four corner beds.

The principal period flowers — candytuft, tulips, peonies and aquilegia — are supplemented with such annuals as blue bachelor buttons and calendulas.

❄❄

Herbs and old-fashioned flowers play a major role on the grounds of scores of house museums scattered throughout New England.

Among the more outstanding is the seventeenth century garden at the *John Whipple House* in Ipswich, Massachusetts, one of the oldest buildings standing in New England and one of the finest examples of seventeenth century architecture. The house, with its steeply pitched roof and casement windows, remained in the Whipple family for more than two hundred years. The west half was built between 1638 and 1640, and the east half of the house was built in 1670.

In 1898, the Ipswich Historical Society bought and restored the house. Many of the old Ipswich families contributed to the furnishings which are of the seventeenth and eighteenth centuries.

The garden, located at the front entrance to the house, was designed by Arthur A. Shurcliff, the noted landscape architect, who was responsible for the Governor's Palace Garden at Williamsburg, Virginia. It was planted by Mrs. A. W. Smith, an author and a member of the Ipswich Garden Club, with materials for which there is documentary evidence in early records.

Mrs. Smith prepared a leaflet, "The Seventeenth Century Garden of the Whipple House," distributed at the Whipple House, in which she wrote:

In the Whipple House Garden we have attempted only to present a collection of the plants most commonly grown in the seventeenth century. Several old favorites, such as burdock, we have left in the waste place to which disuse banished it. Others, equally rank-growing, we have included because they were mentioned so often — comfrey, elecampane, agrimony.

Lavender grows well, although John Josselyn said it did not do well in Maine. Our roses are gallicas and damasks with a history of their being brought from England. And in honor of Anne Bradstreet, poet, wit and wise Puritan, who lived for a time in Ipswich, we give prominent place to the plants she suggested as a reward for her poems . . . "Give thyme or parsley wreath. I ask no bayes."

The garden, surrounded by split paling fence, consists of six raised beds, about ten feet square, with clamshell paths. The planting plan is to have a rose bush as a high center in the middle and then concentric circles of various plants to the edges of each bed. Corners are filled with paired-off plantings to give symmetry to the paths.

Arthur Shurcliff, in 1941, was responsible for the design of the garden in another notable house, the *King Hooper Mansion* (1728) in Marblehead, Massachusetts, now the headquarters of the Marblehead Arts Association.

The garden deteriorated with time until 1969 when the Arrangers of Marblehead started a two-year project of restoration. They retained Shurcliff's general plan, which included square and rectangular plots with box edging, but altered the nature of some of the plant materials.

Within two of the box-bordered beds, the architect used eighteenth century varieties of forget-me-nots, tulips, foxgloves and pinks. Within two larger beds, he planned grassy plots. All four beds are now planted with spirea, with daffodil, tulip and narcissus bulbs for early bloom, and with zinnias for summer color.

The Arrangers planted dogwoods, azaleas and andromeda in corners and along a fence. They also included a small kitchen herb garden with lovage, mint, tansey, wild marjoram, angelica, basil and sage.

❦

A seventeenth century garden is maintained at the *General Sylvanus Thayer Birthplace* in Braintree, Massachusetts, a home restored by the Braintree Historical Society.

The home was built in 1720 but is typically a house of the seventeenth century New England. Even though Sylvanus Thayer, whom the preservation honors, was born there in the late eighteenth century, the whole spirit of the house and garden belongs to the earlier period.

The plan for the garden was formulated by Mrs. A. W. Smith, who planted the garden at the Whipple House, in 1961. Members of the

Braintree Garden Club and Braintree Historical Society cooperated in the planting and care of the beds.

The planting was modified in order to accommodate crowds in the yard and the gardening powers of the caretakers. It was not possible to have a flourishing vegetable garden, which every old house had to have. The flowers, shrubs, trees and herbs are representative, adding charm and revitalization to the whole house.

The design of the herb beds is simply two right-angled triangles with an open side facing the yard. Two sides are fourteen feet long, and the third side is a gentle curve. Other beds are shallow around the house and at one corner of the yard. The side opposite the house is a rough bank which provides ample space for the many perennials.

The herb garden has thirty-six varieties, including all categories from fragrance and culinary to repellents. Industrial herbs include horehound, flax, teasel, hop vine and scouring reed. For fragrance, there is lavender, clove pinks, heliotrope and Harrison yellow rose.

❧❦❧

Another colonial garden is that at *Mission House* in Stockbridge, Massachusetts. The house was built in 1739 by the Reverend John Sergeant, a pioneer missionary in days when

THE COLONIAL GARDENS AT MISSION HOUSE, STOCKBRIDGE, MASSACHUSETTS

Stockbridge was a frontier town, and is now a museum of colonial life. The house, with its beamed ceilings and sharply pitched roof, was moved from Prospect Hill nearby to Main Street by the philanthropist, Miss Mabel Choate in 1926–1927. It was presented to The Trustees of Reservations in 1948.

The garden was originally designed by the late Fletcher Steele, a Boston landscape architect, who devoted eighteen years to planning, moving and laying out the Mission House and its museum rooms, barns and colonial garden. In part, the garden was revised and replanted by Mrs. G. Douglas Krumbhaar in 1962.

Small gardens at the front of the house are bisected by a stone walk which leads to the house entrance. Oval beds on each side of the walk are planted with lavender and alyssum, and are encircled by a brick walk. A host of plants, including hollyhocks, phlox, spirea, peonies and artemesia, crowd the perimeters of both gardens.

More extensive gardens are at the side of the house. Broad walks separate a dozen planting areas. Bordering the long central path on both sides are parallel lines of lamb's ears. Between the lamb's ears is a ground cover of ajuga, primroses, house leeks and, in the early spring, scilla and grape hyacinth bloom under the trees. Madonna lilies are in the center of the borders in the front and in the back are iris, bleeding heart, clary sage and savory.

Planting along the cypress fence includes native wild flowers, ferns and shrubs, yellow lady's-slippers, strawberry shrubs, viburnum and trillium. Four beds comprise a salad garden, while a rose bed is devoted to such old-fashioned shrub roses as old pinks, Empress Josephine, Nuits de Young, and Rose de Resht.

✻✻

Two Presidents and four generations of a distinguished American family lived in the *Old House*, the *Adams National Historic Site* in Quincy, Massachusetts. The five-acre site, administered by the National Park Service, was given to the federal government by the Adams Memorial Society in 1946.

Its seventeen-room mansion and its period garden reflect the way of life of John Adams, first Vice President and second President of the United States, and his descendants. Its rooms hold treasures Adams accumulated during service for the country, and its garden still holds a York rose, brought from England by his wife, Abigail, in 1788.

Other treasures and portraits were added by his son, John Quincy Adams, sixth President, and by his grandson, Charles Francis Adams, appointed by President Lincoln as Minister to Great Britain. Still others were acquired by the fourth generation, John, Charles Francis Jr., Henry and Brooks, all distinguished in either politics or letters.

The house itself represents three architectural styles. The oldest portion was built in 1731 by Major Leonard Vassall, a wealthy West Indian sugar planter. An addition was built by President John Adams in 1800 and, in 1869, Charles Francis Adams added thirty feet to the kitchen ell for servants' quarters, and the following year built the stone library overlooking his grandmother's garden.

A wall today encircles the five acres which are a small part of the original Adams estate.

THE QUINCY, MASSACHUSETTS, RESIDENCE OF PRESIDENT JOHN ADAMS AND HIS DESCENDANTS

A visitor enters gates and follows a straight path to the three-story house with its slate roof. Tall lilacs and vines almost obscure a front porch through which visitors enter for a tour.

The grounds, like the house, have plantings which mirror the tastes of each generation. In addition to the York rose, you can still find a hedge and a magnolia planted by Abigail Adams in the late eighteenth century. John Quincy Adams was proud of the tree museum he established, particularly his collection of nut trees. The grounds still hold enormous elm and black walnut trees that were his. An old orchard has apple, pear, peach and cherry trees.

But the major garden area at the side of the house is a semi-formal English garden, planted by Mrs. Charles Francis Adams about 1850. It consists of rectangles of lawn, with enormous flower borders about each. The rectangles are bisected by walks and crosswalks.

The gardens are planted and maintained just as Mrs. Adams might have done so during the nineteenth century. The gardeners shun hybrids and use only old-fashioned varieties of the more than one hundred flowers they set in every year.

The three-season garden yields spring color with iris, lilac, lemon lilies, and bleeding heart. Later touches of color are provided by zinnias, nicotiana, phlox, blue salvia, spider plant, and marigolds. The fall season will bring on dahlias, and michaelmas daisies. Vines along the house and the nearby stone library include wisteria, old French grape, Dutchman's pipe, and the Virginia creeper.

There are also peonies, day lilies and iris planted by members of the family before 1927. Both house and garden reflect a casual elegance. They are comfortable and not pretentious, existing in quiet harmony.

❋❋

The Adams National Historic Site is located along a much-traveled road close to the heart of crowded and bustling Quincy. Another house with its historic garden, the *Wadsworth-Longfellow House*, has an equally improbable location in the downtown shopping center of Portland, Maine. The three-story brick house is wedged in between a department store and a bank.

The house, best known for its association with poet Henry Wadsworth Longfellow, was built in 1785–1786 by General Peleg Wadsworth, an officer of the Massachusetts militia during the Revolution.

Henry Wadsworth Longfellow lived there during his infancy, boyhood and young manhood and often visited during his later life. He considered the house his home until 1843, a period of thirty-five years.

The fifteen-room residence was the home of the Wadsworth and Longfellow families for one hundred fifteen years. It came into the possession of the Maine Historical Society in June, 1901, by the gift of Anne Longfellow Pierce, a younger sister of Henry Wadsworth Longfellow.

In 1923, the Longfellow Garden Club was formed for the purpose of restoring the badly neglected gardens and raising money for the work. It has done a superb job, retaining old trees and trying to make it the garden Longfellow knew and loved.

The garden is a long and narrow one, hemmed in on one side by an ivy-covered brick wall and by adjacent buildings on the other. Visitors enter the garden from a trellised stoop at the rear of the house. They face a long colonial brick walk that leads to the foot of the garden and an ornamental iron seat.

There are twenty-two individual planting plots, along with such accessories as a fountain, benches placed here and there, and a sundial. The main pathway is lined by border plots made colorful, in turn, with tulips, jonquils, iris, peonies, lilies, monkshood and poppies.

In unexpected corners are patches of johnny-jump-up, sweet spice pinks, and forget-me-nots, together with annuals. Two lateral paths embrace a grassy area, shaded by lilac and mock orange shrubs. On the left, as one leaves the house, is a fragrant grapevine and, outside of the den window, there is the syringa so often mentioned in family journals.

The garden is a wealth of plant varieties

compressed in a comparatively small area. Here in season are lilies of the valley, lemon and plantain lilies, solomon's seal, yellow and peacock violets, periwinkle and trillium, interspersed with ferns. Friends have provided brier roses, whose ancestors flourished and faded here.

The garden is to be as much admired as a period piece as the house.

❈❈❈

Another equally historic house and garden is the *Moffatt-Ladd House* in historic Portsmouth, New Hampshire, which has more than its share of colonial and federal mansions open to the public.

The house was built in 1763 by Captain John Moffatt and lived in by General William Whipple, a relation and a signer of the Declaration of Independence. The house remained in the hands of descendants until 1913 when it was leased for its protection at nominal rent to the Society of Colonial Dames in New Hampshire. The National Society of the Colonial Dames of America in the State of New Hampshire acquired full title to the house in 1969 and maintains it as a museum.

The garden represents the creation of Alexander Hamilton Ladd, who fell heir to the house in 1862. Lawns and flower beds cover more than an acre and a half, and many trees, shrubs, vines and plants are very old. The Society of Colonial Dames tries, in adding perennials and annuals, to use old-fashioned flowers of appropriate kinds.

The yard still has a magnificent horse-chestnut tree planted by General Whipple. It still has lawn areas and curved paths laid out by Alexander Ladd.

Ladd planted wisteria on the western wall of the house and created grass steps leading to the upper level of the garden. He imported bulbs from Holland of tulip, narcissus, crocus, and scilla, of which many survive. These features remain his legacy, along with an occasional fruit tree on the lawn and a line of beehives at the far end against a wall of shrubbery. The dense green wall, with trees and many lilacs, surrounds the entire garden.

The garden consists of a series of terraces with flower beds raised to various heights above the path and banked with turf. On one terrace stands a sundial which once graced the garden of the Earl of Ranfurley in County Tyrone, Ireland. To the left of that terrace, a cross path leads to the original herb garden, which has been expertly replanted.

In 1932, in commemoration of the bicentennial of the birth of George Washington, a scion of the Washington Elm in Cambridge was planted on a higher terrace. Displays of color are provided by lilac hedges and flowering shrubs in May, peonies and roses in June, and a succession of bloom in the beds throughout summer and fall.

❈❈❈

Consider the restoration of the *Harriet Beecher Stowe House and Garden* in Hartford, Connecticut. The famed author, abolitionist and humanitarian lived in that gothic cottage for twenty-three years, from 1873 to her death in 1896. It is the only homestead of the author of *Uncle Tom's Cabin* that has survived either the wrecker's ball or the infringement of changing times.

The restoration was made possible by funds

provided by the late Miss Katharine Seymour Day, a grandniece of Harriet Beecher Stowe. Almost literally, no stone was left unturned by the Stowe-Day Foundation in the restoration of the eight-room house and garden, beginning in 1964.

A wealth of materials provided documentation for architectural features and furnishings. Personal letters of Mrs. Stowe were examined along with period photographs and newspaper articles. Careful sifting of dirt and debris provided bits of tile and sections of plaster moldings. Carpets and matting were reproduced from fragments and photographs.

The research for the gardens was done by Mrs. Holly Stevenson, landscape architect. She took great care to select only flowers and shrubs which had been introduced no later than the period during which Mrs. Stowe lived there.

From Mrs. Stowe's own letters and three articles about the house written when she lived there, it was determined there had been an oval bed in the back yard. Mrs. Stevenson had test borings made to determine the specific location of this garden and its shape.

There was evidence of a cobblestone gutter along the south side of the house, which the Foundation reconstructed. A number of nineteenth century photographs showed a two-rail wooden fence, which was faithfully reproduced.

The same photos also indicated a forked white birch in front of the house, and Mrs. Stevenson carefully found a birch tree of the same configuration. Many of the roses in the round bed on the north side are the Duchess of Sutherland species. It seemed appropriate to have this type of rose since Mrs. Stowe was a friend of the duchess and was entertained by her on several occasions.

As spring turns to summer, and summer to autumn, the flowers that Harriet Beecher Stowe was so fond of will continue to blossom and brighten the grounds of the home where she lived longer than any other place, and where she peacefully died at the age of eighty-five.

CHAPTER 5
SPECIALIZED
GARDENS

Specialized gardens in New England are, by and large, the creation of a couple or a single individual. These are the rose fanciers, the hybridizers, the persons whose green thumb enthusiasm centers on a limited facet of the plant world.

Such a garden is one developed by Mr. and Mrs. Eugene W. Ureneff in Rockland, Maine, whose specialty is the begonia. The couple began developing their private garden in 1952 and opened it to the public during summer months about ten years ago.

Theirs is a sunken garden in a wild natural setting with a brook running through the center. There are forty-eight of the standard type and fourteen hanging tuberous begonia plants. The garden is surrounded by birches, oaks and other trees, with a profusion of green ferns and wild flowers in and around the area.

❊❊

Another specialized garden is the extensive plantings of rhododendrons on the seventy-six acre grounds of the *Heritage Plantation* in the historic Cape Cod village of Sandwich, Massachusetts.

The rhododendrons start their spectacular blooming season about the time the museum opens its gates on May 1 and continue blooming through mid-June. Garden clubs and tourists alike have scheduled trips to Sandwich each year to view the magenta-, champagne-, white-, and orange-hued blossoms, many of which embellish ancient shrubs standing as tall as a house.

❊❊

While Heritage Plantation opened as a diversified museum of Americana in 1969, the

RHODODENDRONS IN FULL BLOOM AT HERITAGE PLANTATION, IN THE CAPE COD VILLAGE OF SANDWICH

49

stands of rhododendrons flourished for long years before under the dedicated care of one man. That man was Charles O. Dexter, noted horticulturist and originator of the famous Dexter rhododendrons.

Dexter, a New Bedford textile manufacturer, bought the seventy-six acres bordering the shores of Upper Shawme Lake in 1921 when he was sixty years old. He built a home there and turned his attention to planting his new estate.

With the help of Paul Frost, a Boston landscape architect, he arranged to have carloads of rhododendrons, mountain laurel, carolina hemlocks and other plants shipped from North Carolina.

His attention turned increasingly to rhododendrons. He obtained plants, cuttings and pollen collected in Europe and Asia and concentrated on hybridizing and propagating. Within a few years he was producing between five thousand and ten thousand seedlings a year.

Seeking to improve local stock, Dexter chose parent plants for their fragrance, habit of growth and size of corolla. He succeeded in producing plants with many color variations and improvements in form.

He was aided by American and foreign horticulturists who sent him plants from Japan, China, India and Germany. In turn, Dexter sold or gave away varieties of his own hybrids by the thousands to gardeners all along the eastern seaboard.

After Dexter's death in 1943, the estate was sold and with time hundreds of Dexter's plant creations vanished from the estate.

In 1967, the land was bought by Josiah K. Lilly III for the purpose of creating a museum of early Americana to be dedicated to the memory of his father, Josiah Kirby Lilly Jr., a distinguished collector and philanthropist. Lilly was a former president of Lilly Pharmaceutical Company of Indianapolis, Indiana, and a summer resident of Falmouth, Massachusetts.

Within the plantation complex of buildings, a military museum includes Lilly's collection of nearly two thousand miniature soldiers which cover the years from 1621 to 1900, and his collection of antique firearms.

The plantation has many facets. Antique autos are housed in a round stone barn, patterned after a giant structure built by the Shakers in Hancock, Massachusetts, in 1826. Nearby is an old restored windmill of Cape Cod origin. An arts and crafts building contains exhibits highlighting the skill of American craftsmen. An old barn houses the museum store.

Aware of the importance of the Dexter grounds, plantation personnel took great pains to preserve the old original Dexter shrubs and sought to place the grounds in the ranks of the best of American gardens.

To this end, the plantation hired Heman A. Howard, horticulturist and former staff member of the Arnold Arboretum, to re-create the gardens. Howard compiled a list of eighty-four known Dexter cultivars and determined that eighteen of these were represented on the grounds.

Howard traveled to arboretums and botanical gardens throughout the east tracking down original Dexter plants and arranging to bring back cuttings or seedlings. He succeeded in bringing back more than seventy-five of the Dexter varieties.

Now the plantation grounds hold more than thirty-five hundred rhododendrons. New plantings were made of azaleas, lilacs, crab apples, mountain ash and many other varieties of flowering trees and shrubs. Existing stands of native pitch pines, black and white oaks, red maples, hollies and beeches have been supplemented with many other trees. As part of the program of redevelopment, trees were labeled for identification.

※※※

The future of the true Dexter rhododendron is indeed bright at Heritage Plantation.

The location of Barrington, Rhode Island, between Providence and the busy resort town of Newport, contributed to heavy and frequent congestion on its narrow, tree-lined streets. Cars and trucks speed only as fast as snail-paced traffic will permit during the summer months. For the knowledgeable visitor, temporary escape from this hustle and bustle is only a few blocks away from the main road.

That escape is *Llys-Yr-Rhosyn*, a private rose garden on slightly more than eleven acres, open to everyone during daylight hours from mid-May to hard fall frosts. The garden, with its more than seventy-five hundred roses, is believed to be the only private rose garden of its size open to the public.

The garden is breathtaking for scents which are heady and subtle, for its broad sweeps of color ranging from the brightest of crimson to the palest of yellow. If you are fortunate during your visit, you will find its owner, Karl P. Jones, riding in his open cart for an inspection of his garden, pruning shears close at hand.

He will tell you, if you ride along with him, that the Welsh name of his estate means "The Royal Court of the Rose," and that he started his extensive garden in 1937 with a two-acre plot and perhaps two hundred roses. The major portion of the property was not developed until his retirement in 1951 from business because of health.

Jones' enthusiasm for plants may be traced to his father, an experimenter with all varieties of flowers. Jones decided to concentrate on roses which, he found, grew well behind his house. One portion of land he acquired had been a school play yard for seventy-five years. It had to be torn up with heavy equipment and took three years to put into proper planting shape. In the fourth year, Jones planted vegetables and, he says, you had to jump to get out of the way as they sprang up.

What you see in the rose area is more than one hundred beds, each of which is about one hundred feet long. You will also find roses alternating with clematis, of which there are more than two hundred that flourish along the perimeter fence.

The more than eleven hundred varieties of roses include early roses which usually bloom about May 20, and hybrid teas which flower from June 5.

Here you will find, among others, the rose Altica, which originated in western China, with its fragile yellow blossoms. The Conrad F. Meyer, a hybrid, is planted along the outside fence. Its large pink blossoms provide color, while its tiny thorns dissuade intruders from making their way through. The entire gable end of the garage near by is covered with Chevy Chase, a red rambler. When it is in bloom, the entire wall is a mass of color to a height of perhaps thirty feet.

What Jones has tried to do, in part, is to preserve some of the old rose varieties he has always loved. One of these is Susan Ball, a very fragrant rose and one which is not on the commercial market now. Another, one of his wife's favorites, is Brandywine which has been off the market for more than twenty-five years. The old-timers include moss roses, galacas, and old shrub roses.

Jones maintains propagating beds in a separate area, importing understock from Germany, Ireland or Canada. He makes a point of grafting dozens of old rose species in order that they may be on hand in his garden.

Jones, along with the gardeners he employs, maintains other garden areas on the grounds. One hill is massed with King Alfred narcissus for a giant splash of yellow in early spring. Azaleas crowd another portion of the hill, which also includes a picnic area. A wild flower garden is carefully nurtured in a wooded area.

The gardens are obviously a labor of love.

❀❀❀

Sun worshipers by the thousands flock each summer to the long stretch of surf-cleansed sand that is Hampton Beach, New Hampshire. They come for the day, the week or the season, and only a small percentage of them take the time to motor a few miles north to an open garden located on a promontory overlooking the sea.

That formal garden in North Hampton is the *Fuller Foundation Gardens*, a memorial to its creator, the late Governor Alvan T. Fuller of Massachusetts.

Fuller began the garden in 1928 on land across the road from his summer mansion. Aware of his wife's love of roses, he turned the site of nearly two acres into a formal rose garden, embellished with other plantings. In 1940, after his death, members of his family endowed the garden to make possible its maintenance as a public showplace.

Roses continue to be the main attraction, and there are more than twenty-five hundred of them. But what began as a rose garden has evolved into a garden with three distinct sections.

The main section is the formal garden, a sunken area with flagstones set along grass paths. Confined by a rectangular hedge of Japanese yews, the garden has borders of the pink Betty Prior rose. It also has perennial borders and thirteen large beds, each with a different variety of rose creating splashes of color from red to off-white.

On the upper level at the head of the garden, a fountain within a circular pool is backed by a stand of rhododendron. To one side, close by the greenhouses in which all plants but the roses are raised, is a garden devoted entirely to roses.

A third area, behind a towering arborvitae hedge, is a rock garden with Oriental touches. Water trickles down a waterfall into a large pool. Tulips in the spring give way to annuals later in the season. Intermingled among other plants are such exotics as tuberous begonias, birds of paradise, fuchsias and lantanas.

A shaded walk has borders of pachysandra, cactus, and white and red patient lucy. Part of the charm of the garden is the unexpected perennial border tucked into one corner and the placement of a concentration of tuberous begonias in another.

It is a fitting memorial for any gardener.

❊❊❊

Another specialized garden is located in the heart of the industrial city of Cranston, Rhode Island, which adjoins Providence. It is the *Winsor Azalea Garden*, open to the public for about three weeks in May when the azaleas are in bloom.

The garden, situated on the shores of Fenner's Pond, was a barren, rather hilly area many years ago. Nearby residents found it convenient, during coal furnace days, to dump their ashes down the forty-five foot incline.

The land was bought as a home site by Mr. and Mrs. Ralph Tilton Winsor in the late 1930s. Their first major task, as home owners, was to eliminate the dump and beautify the area. They placed huge boulders in terraces and planted hundreds of pachysandra to prevent the earth from being washed down and into the pond.

With the boulders in place, they began to design an English rock garden. The death of Winsor's father, who lived across the road, altered their plans. The elder Winsor, a horticultural hobbyist, had on his property masses of azaleas which he had brought from Japan.

The azaleas were transplanted on the former dump site, along with huge fuchsia bushes. The present garden progressed from this beginning to take its present form. The Winsors gradually added flowering crab, cherry, dogwood and evergreens. They also set in roses, perennials and annuals to provide constant color through the growing season.

With the basic planting completed, the couple built a goldfish pool. They realized that pollutants in the adjacent pond might destroy their garden and had a well dug. The water flow from the well, one hundred twenty-five gallons a minute, was such that they added a waterfall to provide another point of landscape interest.

❊❊❊

A garden which received an outstanding distinction award from the National Council of Garden Clubs, as well as the May Duff Walters Church Garden Award, is the *Temple Beth-El Biblical Garden* in Providence, Rhode Island. The garden, formally dedicated in May, 1960, is the creation of Mrs. David C. Adelman, founder and first president of the Eden Garden Club of Temple Beth-El. It is open to visitors from about May 15 to frost.

When Mrs. Adelman was asked to landscape the upper cement patio at the rear of the Temple, she closely inspected the narrow planting strip, a plot sixty feet by two feet in area, which bordered a stone wall.

She was determined that the small and intricate space would give visitors inspiration and tranquility and enough spiritual inquisitiveness to delve deeper into the Bible and into horticultural facts connected with it.

As she progressed, she tagged each plant with the chapter, paragraph or line from the Old Testament which contained a reference to it.

In a pamphlet Mrs. Adelman prepared for the Temple, she wrote:

The central theme of our garden is the stone tablets of the Ten Commandments. They are framed in the branches of a weeping mulberry tree which, with the help of careful pruning, droops in the exact shape of the tablets.

In I Chronicles 14:15, there is the following passage:

"And it shall be, when thou shalt hear the sound of going in the mulberry trees, that then thou shalt go out to battle, for God has gone out before thee to smite the hosts of the Philistines."

This seems to me to be the central theme of all of our lives, the prayer that God will go before us and protect us from evil. However, I take a broader view and interpret the lines to mean the evil of present-day dictators. I hope that this symbol will be an omen of this prayer.

The mulberry tree is considered the wisest tree of all. It does not put forth its buds until all vestiges of frost are gone. Then, they all seem to pop simultaneously and you can hear this small explosion. This is what was meant by I Chronicle's ... "sound of going in the mulberry trees" ... God chose this season to insure comfortable weather for His soldiers.

On each side of the theme, Mrs. Adelman shaped firethorn, or pyracantha, to espalier in the form of the seven-branched candelabras, known as menorahs.

She wrote, " 'Thorn' is a name given to almost any plant in the Bible which has sharp needle-like extensions from its stems. I chose the firethorn for this reason, and for the additional reason that although fruit trees are the only other trees that espalier easily, they are objectionable because they bring insects and spoiled fruit."

The ground cover includes myrtle through which saffron crocuses come up in the spring. Among herbs in the garden are rue, wormwood and sage. A willow tree is planted at one corner of the terrace and a mountain ash at the other.

Bittersweet vines, though not biblical plants, are trained along the rock wall in the shape of angels' wings. In a small square of broken rock, Mrs. Adelman planted the burning bush, or winged euonymus Alatus, its red transparent berries providing color in the fall. The broken rock symbolizes the destruction by Moses of the first tablets containing the Ten Commandments as he descended the mountain and saw his people worshiping the golden calf.

※※

At Harvard University in Cambridge, Massachusetts, is a garden which uses nature as a model rather than a medium and which may be of interest to garden lovers. That garden is the Ware Collection of *Blaschka Glass Models of Plants* in the university's Botanical Museum.

The collection, which attracts more than two hundred thousand visitors a year, contains 784 life-size models representing some 780 species and varieties of plants in 164 families. It also includes 3218 detailed models of enlarged flowers and anatomical sections of plants.

The collection serves as a tool in the study of botany and is used by students of Harvard, Radcliffe, and other colleges in the Boston area. Students come to study the three-dimensional models of plant life, ranging from the lowest forms to the most highly specialized.

The concept of glass models of plant life as a teaching aid occurred to Professor George Lincoln Goodale, founder and first director of the Botanical Museum.

In 1886, four years before the museum building was completed, he chanced upon glass models of marine animals in Harvard's Museum of Comparative Zoology. He liked them and

SOME OF BLASCHKA GLASS MODELS OF PLANTS IN HARVARD'S BOTANICAL MUSEUM

journeyed to Dresden, Germany, to talk with their creators, Leopold Blaschka and his son, Rudolph.

The Blaschkas were persuaded to make a few models of plants. Those models were of such fine quality that Mrs. Elizabeth C. Ware of Boston and her daughter, Miss Mary Lee Ware, agreed to finance continued botanical work by the Blaschkas. They continued that financial support through the lifetime of both artisans and presented the entire collection to Harvard

as a memorial to Dr. Charles Eliot Ware of the Class of 1834.

In 1890, the Blaschkas concentrated all their time on plant models. They worked together until Leopold's death in 1895. Son Rudolph carried on the work until 1936, three years before his death.

In the beginning, the two men found plant materials in the Royal Gardens at Pilnitz, Germany, and in their own garden which contained both North American and European species of plants. They broadened the collection by obtaining plants from the botanical gardens in Berlin and Dresden.

Rudolph made two trips in 1892 and 1895 to western and southeastern portions of the United States to collect and sketch plants. The end result was the creation of models, faithful in every detail and color, which provide a panoramic exhibit of plant evolution.

Among the thousands of detailed models are three special exhibits. One is a group of cryptogams, illustrating the life history of fungi, bryophytes and ferns. A second group of sixty-four models depicts fungal diseases of fruits. The third group charts the relationship of insects to the transfer of pollen.

* * *

Raised flower beds and plant labels in braille are two features of a garden established primarily for the blind in Providence, Rhode Island. It is located along a busy thoroughfare behind a brick building which serves as headquarters for the Rhode Island Association for the Blind.

The garden site was nothing but rubble in a former house foundation when the association took over a vacant manufacturing plant in 1964 as its new quarters. A garden club, the Dirt Gardeners of Providence, suggested that a garden in the cellar location might be an oasis for both staff and visitors.

The association was delighted with the idea. It asked only that the garden not be called a fragrance garden or a garden for the blind. As a result, a plaque within the garden states it is a garden for the blind and their sighted friends.

The Dirt Gardeners raised funds for the project and hired Raymond W. Thayer, a landscape architect to design the garden. It was opened with formal dedication services on May 16, 1968.

The garden, protected by a high wire fence, is a rectangle about thirty feet by sixty feet. A terrace at the driveway level consists of a lawn area with a broad walk and picnic tables. The planting is confined to the perimeter.

Seven broad steps with heavy handrails lead to the garden proper with gravel walks between raised flower beds formed with railroad ties. There are benches for relaxation and plant materials chosen for texture and fragrance as well as color.

The raised beds, easily accessible to touch, hold a great variety of fragrant herbs, such as peppermint and thyme, along with flowering plants such as marigolds and geraniums. Wild roses, such as the Betty Prior, were chosen for their fragrance. Bushes and evergreens, chosen for texture and for a range of green color, are grouped along the perimeter, completely screening the fence.

The garden is used as a teaching aid during the warm weather months. Staff members find it an excellent tool in teaching both teenage and pre-school youngsters about plant life.

CHAPTER 6
SOME
HOUSE MUSEUM
GARDENS

There are more than three hundred house museums open to the public in the six New England states. These are homes ranging in time from colonial days into the twentieth century, which are being preserved as cherished facets of American life.

Some are lacking in garden areas. Many have gardens which have been restored to the period of the houses. Some are token gardens, such as one at the *Parker Tavern* in Reading, Massachusetts.

❈❈

That token garden, a project of the Reading Garden Club, was planted only after careful research. It is meant to suggest the things a farm wife of about 1800 would grow for food, seasonings, medicine, poisons, cloth (flax), dyestuffs, soap, scents, and just plain "pretties."

It consists of a narrow strip, informal in character, across the front of the 1694 saltbox house. With the exception of black-eyed susans, the plants were practically all originally brought or sent over from the Old World where they were used for the same purposes. In addition, there are the old-time shrubs, the common lilac and syringa, plus the small cornelian cherry tree.

❈❈

The token garden has its story to tell of early living as much as any of the furnishings in the house. Like them, what was once used as a necessity often has changed its function to being decorative today.

Some house gardens are in the process of restoration, like two which are the property of The Society for the Preservation of New England Antiquities, with its headquarters in Boston.

The *Codman House* in Lincoln, Massachusetts, is a nineteenth and early twentieth century estate with formal gardens, including a pool and statuary. The gardens, which have been largely overgrown in recent years, are being gradually restored by a resident overseer.

The *Bown House* (Roseland Cottage) in Woodstock, Connecticut, had a formal garden in an estate layout of the nineteenth century. The garden is only partially kept up by a caretaker. The hope of the society is to put it in topnotch condition, perhaps with the aid of a local garden club.

A third property of the society, *Lyman House* in Waltham, Massachusetts, has impressive grounds in the layout of a nineteenth century estate. Its large lawns and giant rhododendrons are a tranquil retreat close to the heart of the city. But what is most striking are the historic greenhouses at the rear of the residence.

The estate, named *The Vale*, was the country seat of Theodore Lyman, merchant. Built in 1793, it remained the home of the Lyman family until 1951 when it was deeded to the society.

The house itself incorporates three styles of architecture. Two-story core of the house was designed by Samuel McIntire, master carver of Salem, in the federal style. The mansion was enlarged and remodeled during the 1880s in the Victorian style. In 1917, colonial touches were made to a number of the original rooms by removing Victorian overlay and replacing forms.

The land, which now consists of thirty acres, was laid out with the help of William Bell, an English gardener, after the manner of Humphrey Repton. Repton, an Englishman, believed in open vistas and a naturalistic style of landscape design.

Lawns were extended, vistas were opened through woods, and a brook was dammed to form a pond. An informal pleasure garden was planted at the rear of the house. Shrubs and ornamental trees were scattered about in abundance. And a large greenhouse was built in 1804.

An inventory of the plant material at The Vale is indicative of the grand manner in which the estate was planned. There are thirty-seven varieties of trees, some with a spread of about one hundred feet. There are twenty-eight types of shrubs, including three varieties of rhododendron, and five varieties of vines.

The original brick greenhouse is divided in two sections, and the only part glassed in is that half facing the house. Running the length of the greenhouse in the center is an elaborate system of flues built in a brick wall. The flues remained closed while a large wood fire blazed and smoked. Once the smoke dissipated, the flues were opened to permit heat throughout the glassed-in area.

Theodore Lyman is said to have cultivated fruits of many kinds, including bananas and pineapples, with the aid of this heating system. The greenhouse today contains a massive Hamburg grapevine, grown from a clipping brought from Hampton Court in England about 1870. Its thick and ancient branches, supported by wires, still yield clusters of muscat grapes.

A second greenhouse is devoted to scores of camellia shrubs grown in wooden planters. A third greenhouse, the *Kathryn S. Taylor Greenhouse*, serves as a teaching center for the Massachusetts Horticultural Society.

✳✳✳

Gardens of more recent vintage are those at *Naumkeag*, a summer estate in Stockbridge, Massachusetts, and a property of The Trustees of Reservations.

Naumkeag, an Indian word for *haven of peace*, was built in 1886 by Joseph Hodges Choate, a native of Salem, Massachusetts, a wealthy New York attorney, and Ambassador to the Court of St. James's in London for six years.

The twenty-six-room, Norman style mansion was designed by Stanford White, the noted architect, and erected on the west side of Prospect Hill, facing the ridge of Monument Mountain across the Housatonic River.

The original gardens on the steep site were designed by Nathaniel F. Barrett, a Boston landscape architect. He created a flower garden with beds of herbaceous flowers and of annuals, divided by gravel paths. He also installed two broad lawn terraces.

Mrs. Choate, smitten by the Unter den Linden walk in Berlin during a visit to Germany, later had her own linden walk of sixty trees planted straight through the estate. The lindens now are towering.

After her parents' death, Miss Mabel Choate inherited the estate. A gardening enthusiast, she expanded garden areas and made many innovations until her own death in 1958.

Miss Choate wrote in a privately printed booklet, "Naumkeag Garden," in 1956:

When I inherited the place, I discovered that there was no spot to sit out of doors in the shade in the afternoon, for the house faces due west and the afternoon sun is terrific. I had just been to California, where every house has an Outdoor Room, a most delightful retreat and one used for every purpose. This I felt I must have, and the southern corner of the house was the only place possible, but a very steep and difficult place to alter.

Just at that moment, Fletcher Steele, distinguished landscape architect of Boston, had come to lecture at the Lenox Garden Club, and it was suggested that he should take a look at Naumkeag. He at once announced that it was useless to do anything until the entrance at the back door was improved.

Looking at it with new eyes, I saw that he was right. It was dreadful. A small circular driveway, too small for anything but horse and buggy, was surrounded by a dilapidated lattice fence. Quickly we got to work, and a high brick wall was made enclosing a large space with paved court, which also gave room for a shady retired spot for hammock and chairs.

Steele's collaboration with Miss Choate was to continue for many years, sparing no expense.

For the outdoor room and afternoon garden, oak pilings rescued from a seventy-five-year submersion in Boston Harbor were carved and colored to resemble Venetian posts. Marble-chip paths were outlined in boxwood, framing four fountains which flow into a black-mirror pool.

The next project was a sloping terrace from the afternoon garden to the linden walk. Fill and loam were trucked in to provide the desired grade. A double hedge of hemlock was planted for privacy along the terraced area, and the bank was covered with ivy and clematis.

The steep site of Naumkeag made possible the next ambitious improvement. This was an elaborate pair of stairs leading from the afternoon garden down the steep banking to a cutting garden far below. The climb down was made easier on each parallel stairway by forming four platforms along the way. A basin was placed at each platform level. A watercourse was fashioned between the matching pair of stairs, permitting water to trickle from the black glass pool in the afternoon garden down into basins at each level. What is now known as the fountain steps is perhaps the most impressive facet of the Naumkeag gardens.

With time, tree peonies and a rock garden took the place of lawn terraces. An evergreen garden was planted with broad-leafed evergreens and dwarf pines.

The garden took on new dimensions after Miss Choate visited the Orient in 1935. She brought back with her scores of marble figures and carvings. These included Buddhas, lions, dogs, and an ancient rock on a Ming pedestal.

With Steele's help, these were made a part of a Chinese garden, its focal point a Chinese open-fronted house which resembles a temple. Features within the sizable garden are authentic. It has ginkgo trees, a pink brick wall and stone lions guarding the temple steps. In one corner a marble table is circled by marble-covered stools.

These are highlights of the gardens of Naumkeag, reputed to be among the loveliest in America.

✳✳✳

A second property of The Trustees of Reservations has extensive gardens of another kind. That is the *Stevens-Coolidge Place* in North Andover, Massachusetts.

Part of an original grant from the Massachusetts Bay Colony to John Stevens in 1645,

the estate remained in the same family for eight generations. Its last occupants were the Honorable and Mrs. John G. Coolidge.

Mrs. Coolidge, the former Helen S. Stevens, lived in "The Home Place" until 1962. Mr. Coolidge, born in 1863, was an author and a diplomat who served his country for many years in China, as Secretary of the United States Embassy in Mexico, and as United States Minister to Nicaragua.

The original portion of the house was built around 1800 and served as a tavern in the 1820s and 1830s. It was restored in colonial revival style and is an elegant example of the decorative arts of the first quarter of the twentieth century.

On the eighty-nine-acre estate, mixed hardwoods — sugar maples, shag bark hickory, and oak — many planted as many as one hundred fifty years ago, fringe the field areas. The grounds are a grand mix of sweeping green lawns, rich pasture land and, closer to the house, a series of individual gardens.

A brick terrace at the rear of the house commands a view of all garden areas. The terrace is furnished with wicker tables and chairs, with pots of geraniums and hydrangeas, and with pieces of Chinese pottery.

In the distance, lawns in an orchard are well manicured. To one side, giant willow trees spread huge limbs and leafy branches over a series of greenhouses and cold frames. Also in the distance, a row of tall Alberta spruce parallels a serpentine brick wall.

A lawn sloping from the terrace ends at a sunken garden enclosed by granite walls. The garden is entered through wrought iron gates, flanked by stone posts, atop which are black metal urns. That garden for all seasons has a profusion of lilacs, phlox, and late spring peonies. Clematis and climbing roses cling to the walls. Many varieties of fuchsias crowd the corners, and hibiscus flourishes in pots. Colorful perennials blend with thyme, marjoram and other herbs in borders.

Close by, a second garden area is enclosed by a privet hedge. This one has large beds of both annuals and perennials in what could easily be a cutting garden.

❈❈❈

An even grander mansion and garden is *Eolia*, located in Harkness Memorial State Park in Waterford, Connecticut, a few miles from New London.

The two hundred thirty-five acre estate with its forty-two room Italian style mansion was the home of Mr. and Mrs. Edward S. Harkness who bestowed more than $200 million on various philanthropies. Harkness was the heir to a fortune initiated through heavy investment by his father, Stephen Harkness, in John D. Rockefeller's Standard Oil Co.

The villa, begun in 1902, is a three-story

THE MANSION AND GARDENS OF EOLIA, HARKNESS MEMORIAL STATE PARK, WATERFORD, CONNECTICUT

limestone structure built on a promontory overlooking the sea. During their marriage, the couple added twenty-six other buildings including several cottages, a large greenhouse, livestock barns, living quarters for the help, and a clubhouse for bowling, billiards and squash.

Mrs. Harkness, concerned about the effects of infantile paralysis on children, in 1920 remodeled one estate building into a recuperation and rehabilitation center for youngsters discharged from the New York Orthopedic Hospital. That program continued until 1943 when Coastal Defense installed gun emplacements on the shore of the estate for the protection of the submarine base at New London.

At her death in June, 1950, Mrs. Harkness left the estate to the State of Connecticut to be used in a manner beneficial to public health.

Today, about half of the estate serves as a private recreation area for Connecticut's handicapped. It has overnight cottages for handicapped individuals, a dining hall and kitchen, and schoolrooms for pre-school cerebral palsy victims.

The other half of the park is open to visitors on a year-round basis. The elegant mansion with its large rooms and high ceilings serves as a gallery for the Rex Brasher collection of eight hundred seventy-four bird paintings, bought by the state in 1941 for $74,900. The grounds with their Italian formal gardens are open for picnics or for strolling.

Vine-covered porticos at the side of the house look out over a series of gardens and the sea beyond. The gardens, planted in part from the ample greenhouse on the grounds, bloom from early spring until the killing frosts of autumn.

Trees and shrubs are geometrically shaped in a topiary garden. Rectangles of lawn are set off by boxwood hedges. There are large urns with petunias and other annuals, placed at strategic points, along with statuary.

A sizable side garden concentrates largely on roses and beds of heliotrope. A rock garden flourishes on a lower level and, close by the gardens, the limbs of a Japanese maple shelter five small gravestones marking the final homes for the Irish terriers which were family pets.

Away from the house, a long path flanked by luxurious flower borders leads to a series of connected greenhouses. Park personnel still maintain exotic plants here. There are, among other things, grape vines more than sixty years old, camellia trees from Mexico, tuberous begonias, banana plants and cacti.

❋❈❋

Many of the house museum gardens are fairly small. All, however, are individual. In infinite variety, all reflect the eras in which the houses were built. Here are some examples.

In Concord, Massachusetts, the *Orchard House* in which Louisa May Alcott wrote *Little Women*, was built in 1650 with a 1730 addition. Its furnishings and its grounds, however, reflect the Victorian era during which Louisa May was an occupant.

Apple trees and tall lilacs are much in evidence on the grounds. To augment the plantings, Mrs. Mary R. Fenn, the Orchard House board member in charge of the grounds, took a creative approach. Writing in the news letter, "New England Wild Flower Notes," Spring, 1972, of the New England Wild Flower Society, she said:

Planning a garden at a historic house which is open to the public is by no means the same as planning one's own garden. Existing plants and shrubs must be dealt with; it must be a minimum-care garden with no nonsense about using temperamental plants which need lifting and storing during winter; no bushes must obscure windows for this encourages vandalism. And of course it must be in keeping with the period of the house.

Several years ago my daughter, Miss Mary Gail, and I decided to do something about the garden at Orchard House. There is indeed an apple orchard on the sloping lawn, but the old garden had become a jungle of hosta plants.

When we began thinning them out, we had a delightful surprise, for underneath all of those leaves were jack-in-the-pulpits, stone crop, violets, lily-of-the-valley and beds of myrtle. Bronson Alcott often took his "little women" off for walks in the woods for wild flowers, and surely they must have planted some in their garden.

We like to think the plants we found are descendants of the Alcotts' flowers. To get in to see these treasures, we made little paths, bordered with bricks we found on the place.

Soon the townspeople dropped in to see what was going on, and they began to bring us wild flowers too — yellow violets, forget-me-nots, phlox, beebalm, false Solomon's seal. So the garden grew. The bushes are now at a reasonable height. The wild flowers are multiplying, and the tourists enjoy walking along the little paths beneath tall trees. Best of all, it pretty much takes care of itself.

❄❄❄

In North Bennington, Vermont, the *Governor McCullough Mansion* is a large, white clapboard Victorian house which stands centered among its tall trees and landscaped grounds of about three acres.

Built in 1902, it was later the home of John G. McCullough who became governor of Vermont in 1902. The mansion is now under the care of the McCullough Mansion Association, an organization which, at the request of the McCullough family, seeks to preserve the historic site for future generations as well as promote its use for educational, community, artistic and intellectual pursuits.

The small formal garden to the north of the mansion, which has both annual and perennial beds, would take only a short examination on the part of a visitor although its accouterments include a garden seat, sundial and a granite bird bath half hidden in the shade of flowering trees and shrubs. Thirty trees representing twenty-five species have been marked with numbers to form a tree tour surrounding the mansion. The key to the tree tour is a descriptive booklet available at the house.

But the real beauty of the gardens and surrounding lawns is the way they enhance the mansion. An early photograph of the house without any planting shows up the stark lines and gables of the structure. They are softened with the addition of trees, an indication that the landscaping was planned for the future, even one hundred years in the future.

❄❄❄

In Augusta, Maine, the *Blaine House*, circa 1830, is representative of the general design of estates of that period. At the same time, its gardens reflect tastes and plantings of later eras.

The two-story building of classic revival design was the residence of James G. Blaine, who

THE BLAINE HOUSE, AUGUSTA, MAINE

ran for President in 1844 on a platform of anti-rum, anti-Romanism and anti-rebellion. His daughter, Mrs. Harriet Blaine Beale, presented the house to the state in 1919 as a memorial to her son, killed during World War I.

The gardens and grounds are about three acres, divided into a formal garden, private garden, and areas of spacious lawn and shrub borders. Scattered throughout the lawn are many large American elm trees.

The formal garden includes five flower beds, four of which are annual flowers and one a perennial garden with annuals added to give constant color throughout the summer. The annual flowers are of many varieties such as zinnia, marigold, portulaca, sweet alyssum, petunia, torenia, and coleus. The perennials include iris, campanula, phlox, delphinium, oriental poppy, chrysanthemum, and hardy lily.

The private garden is made up mostly of lawn and shrub borders. The borders include many azaleas, rhododendron, roses, Japanese red maple, taxus, and white pine.

Less exotic, but intriguing in its own way, is the garden at the *Cushing House* in Newburyport, Massachusetts, the home of the Historical Society of Old Newbury.

The garden is a perfect companion to the house, a three-story brick structure of federal design. The house was built about 1808 by a sea captain during an era when Newburyport was a bustling center for maritime commerce.

It was bought ten years later by John Cushing and remained in the family until 1956. It was given to the historical society by Cushing heirs and is now a museum open to the public.

Caleb, the son of John Cushing, was responsible for the design of the original garden, one which the historical society has sought to restore. Caleb, a statesman and the first envoy to China from the United States, admired a garden design during a visit to France and brought it back with him in 1830.

While retaining the formal pattern of flower or rose beds in squares and circles, he added wild flowers found in New England woods to give the garden a domestic flavor.

He placed the garden to one side of the house, screened it from the street with board fencing and built a pagoda-roofed garden house at the head of the garden.

Portions of the garden were overgrown and much of the original design was lost as a consequence at the time the historical society took over the house. Painstaking research resulted in the present restoration.

CHAPTER 7
PARKS AND OTHER PUBLIC PLACES

A memorial rose garden in a city park, a meditation chapel garden in the pines, and an arboretum in a cemetery. The variety of gardens is broad indeed in New England's parks and other public places.

The *Norwich Memorial Garden* covers a two-acre tract within Mohegan Park in Norwich, Connecticut. The rose garden was conceived and brought to fruition by the late Roy D. Judd, a one-time member of the city's Park Board and a lover of roses.

Judd, in 1946, led a drive to create the garden as a memorial to those who gave their lives and in honor of those who served during World War II. He donated funds of his own and enlisted support from members of the Rotary Club, other citizens and other organizations.

With more than $20,000 on hand for the project, the city chose a rocky site within the park for the garden. The garden became a community affair as residents helped to remove some one hundred tons of rock and to spread more than twenty-four hundred yards of loam.

In 1947, the first rose, a Lady Stanhope, was planted. At the time of the dedication of the garden on July 11, 1948, the roses numbered more than three thousand bushes of one hundred seventy-five varieties. The garden consists of two hundred square and circular beds framed by lawn. Architectural interest is provided by a gazebo and a series of latticed arches festooned with climbing roses.

A plaque at the edge of the garden was erected by the Norwich Rotary Club to "the memory of Roy D. Judd who by his leadership and generosity made possible this Norwich Memorial Garden." Judd, at his death, willed

$25,000 to the city as the Judd Memorial Fund to aid in maintenance of the garden.

✻

Roses are the cornerstone around which many park gardens revolve, particularly in Connecticut.

Hartford, Connecticut, claims its garden was the first municipal rose garden in the United States. The garden, located in one hundred-acre *Elizabeth Park*, once the estate of Charles M. Pond, was planted in 1897.

The garden, dominated by a pavilion, covers three acres. It has more than fourteen thousand

ROSES IN ELIZABETH PARK, HARTFORD, CONNECTICUT

roses in nine hundred forty varieties. Nearby is a sixty bed plot with annuals, perennials and a rock garden. There are also four greenhouses with conservatory and tropical plants.

In New Haven, Connecticut, the *Pardee Rose Gardens* cover an area of six acres on the eastern side of East Rock Park. The mountainous park of four hundred forty-six acres includes a peak once used by Indians for smoke signaling.

The rose gardens were built in the early 1920s with money provided under the will of William S. Pardee which directed the Commission of Public Parks "to grow beautiful flowers in memory of my mother and sister."

The predominant plantings are roses of some fifty varieties, but there are beds of seasonal flowers that vary with the season from spring flowers to asters and chrysanthemums. The western edge of the garden is lined with flowering trees. A recent addition to the park is a floral wedding cake on top of which many brides and grooms pose for wedding pictures. The cake is made of tiers or layers of brick, each planted with rose bushes.

Across the park drive from the gardens are the *Pardee Greenhouses* where the Park Department not only cultivates its plants but also where spring, fall and Christmas flower shows are held.

In addition to this garden, the city also has *Edgerton Gardens*, the former twenty-five-acre Brewster Estate, which was left to the city and is being developed as an arboretum. The gardens have extensive plantings of dogwood, magnolia, azalea and more than fifty different species of trees.

Another city facility is the *West Rock Nature Center* which covers about fifty acres in West Rock Park. The Nature Center was started in 1947 and is known as the park that children have built. There is a White Oak Club attached to the center, and its members are area youngsters who volunteer an hour of work on the center for every hour of fun and recreation.

The center includes a nature trail with trees and plants identified, a zoo of small wild animals indigenous to the area, and a bird zoo.

Roses are very much a part of the gardens of *Hamilton Park* in Waterbury, Connecticut. The rose garden, which is listed by The All American Rose Selection of Approved Rose Gardens, is in the form of a diamond, covering about 14,400 square feet. The design was planned so that, if added space is needed, more beds could be laid out without disturbing the design.

Some sixty beds contain about two thousand varieties of roses, ranging in color from yellow to orange-red. Each year the Park Department receives, from certain commercial rose growers, a number of experimental roses. These roses are placed in beds which are marked and evaluated.

❧❦❧

The park in historic Portland, Maine, is fifty-three-acre *Deering Oaks*, colloquially called "The Oaks" because of the large number of trees of that species. Its *Rose Circle*, begun in 1930, is about one hundred feet in diameter and is made up of two large circles divided by six paths.

There are eighteen beds, twelve on the outer perimeter and six inner beds, with eight hundred rose bushes of seventy varieties. They in-clude hybrid perpetuals, hybrid teas, grandifloras and floribundas.

The majority of the bedding plants that are started in the park greenhouses are transferred to eighty flower beds throughout the city. They take the place of the twenty-five thousand tulips which bloom each spring until early June.

❧❦❧

There are four large beds of floribunda roses in *Roger Williams Park* in Providence, Rhode Island. These, however, constitute a very small part of extensive gardens.

The core of the park was the property of the Williams family, which built a small summer cottage on it. The cottage, built in 1772, and one-hundred acres of land were left to the city by Betsy Williams in 1872 for park purposes.

The park, now embracing four hundred fifty acres, has a wide range of recreational facilities, including a pond, tennis courts and an amusement complex. It also has a natural history museum and zoo area.

The *Betsy Williams Cottage*, opened as a house museum, has a herb garden of circular beds at its front door. Park personnel maintain floral displays by the main entrance to the park, depicting the American flag and the American Legion emblem.

❧❦❧

The *Charles H. Smith Memorial Greenhouses and Experimental Gardens* within the park have an extensive program throughout the year. The greenhouses are noted for their orchid collection and for their annual Christmas display of poinsettias. The experimental gardens have a variety of ground covers, along with different varieties of crab apple and dogwood.

But the most distinctive area is a Japanese garden, enclosed by fencing of vertical boards. In front of the garden stands a large stone lantern, one of a pair presented in 1954 by the Japanese government to Rhode Island in recognition of the one hundredth anniversary of the opening of western trade by Commodore Matthew C. Perry of Rhode Island.

The garden consists of gentle hills with outcroppings of rock and rounded bridges connecting a series of islands in a lily pond. Trees and shrubs, including Japanese tree peonies, are small in size. Some are pruned to achieve exotic forms, and others are espaliered along the fence.

❉

Boston, Massachusetts, has long been famed for its *Public Garden*. The garden was created in 1859 on the first tract of land formed by filling in the Back Bay. Tourists perhaps know the garden best for the swan boats which ply the three-acre artificial pond during the summer months.

Fine, ancient specimen trees are labeled throughout its twenty-four acres and throughout the forty-eight-acre *Common* across the street. Geometric flower beds are planted to provide blooms from early spring into fall.

Boston also has a splendid rose garden of perhaps two acres on *The Fenway*, adjacent the Boston Museum of Fine Arts. The garden,

BOSTON'S FENWAY ROSE GARDEN, ADJACENT TO THE MUSEUM OF FINE ARTS

maintained by the Parks Department, is enclosed by a hemlock hedge. Its thousands of roses are clustered along borders and in large, formal beds. Roses climb on a series of latticed arches and set off a large pool which contains a fountain.

But what intrigues one about Boston is the unexpected garden project.

An example is a multi-garden area of more than seven acres close by the *Fenway Rose Garden*. Here you will find some three hundred individual gardens, maintained by members of the Fenway Garden Society. Most are a combination of flowers and vegetables. The rest concentrate either on vegetable plots or on flowers and shrubs.

The garden began as a Victory Garden, one of forty tended by Boston residents during World War II. With war's end, a neighborhood group formed the society for the purpose of continuing the gardening as a hobby. The city agreed to give them the use of the land.

❋

Another example is a rooftop garden on the fourteenth floor of the *Suffolk County Courthouse* behind Boston's new Government Center. The garden, open only by appointment, is reached through the office of John E. Powers, clerk of the Supreme Judicial Court of the Commonwealth of Massachusetts.

Powers, an avid gardener, began the garden several years ago on the fifteen-foot wide roof balcony which extends around the fourteenth floor. He built containers from salvaged materials and hauled tons of loam in fifty-pound bags to fill them and to create borders edged with brick.

The flourishing garden now extends for one hundred fifty feet. Tiers of containers form windbreaks at both ends of the garden. Literally thousands of plants are in bloom in season, impervious to high winds and occasional torrential rains. The garden contains most of the flowers you will find in a suburban garden, from dahlias and snapdragons to seventy rose bushes, yielding more than two thousand roses.

Powers uses the garden as an example of what can be planted in an urban environment. That use, demonstrated to neighbors and friends, led to formation of the South Boston Garden Club with three hundred members, the largest in the state, all dedicated to city gardening.

❋

A new garden park is in the making in Boston's Back Bay to take the place of the former Mother Church Park, which was a part of the First Church of Christ, Scientist. The old park consisted of two acres of flowers and shrubs.

The park was eliminated in 1968 when the church began construction of a new *Christian Science Church Center*, a complex of modern church-related buildings, including a twenty-eight-story international headquarters.

While part of the park is now open, it is not expected to be complete until 1974 or later. It will have seven acres of open space between the buildings.

Large red oaks are planted around the rim of the center on Massachusetts and Huntington avenues. A linden tree arcade has already been planted, which extends along the Huntington Avenue side of the property just inside the oaks. This grove of little-leaf lindens, set three abreast, will eventually be trimmed flat on the top and square on the corners. The undersides will be shaped into vaulted arches, forming leaf-covered walkways for strollers.

Beyond the linden arcade, facing the seven hundred-foot long reflecting pool, will be a row of large bench gardens, planted with pink tulips, violet geraniums, white hyacinths, blue aster, orange chrysanthemums, yellow alyssum, and holly.

After sunset, lights placed at root level in the linden tree arcade shine up into the leaved arches, illuminating the entire area. The bench gardens will be lighted by lights set on top of poles, and a fountain at one end of the pool will also be lighted.

Another row of red oaks will be planted along Massachusetts Avenue in front of the entrance to the church. Inside the row of oaks, a thick lawn will extend about eighty feet to meet a red brick walk leading to the new entrance.

A circle of five specimen locust trees, placed to the left front of the church entrance, will offer a counterpoint to the sweep of the domed structure. The circle will be planted with periwinkle and blue crocuses.

✵✻✵

A less formal garden is that of *Cathedral of the Pines* and the *Garden of Remembrance* in Rindge, New Hampshire. The four hundred-acre open air cathedral is an international shrine which has attracted hundreds of thousands of visitors.

The cathedral was the inspiration and creation of Dr. and Mrs. Douglas Sloane, long-time summer residents of Rindge. When a hurricane swept through their land in 1938, they inspected the damage along with their son, Sanderson.

They found the hurricane had felled scores of trees on a thickly wooded knoll, opening up a view of a reservoir below the knoll and of wooded hills, including Mount Monadnock, in the distance. Gazing at the towering spar pines, Sanderson called them cathedral pines. He voiced a wish to build his home there, along with a little chapel.

Sanderson never got his wish. He entered the service when the United States mobilized for World War II. The plane he was piloting on a bombing run was shot down in February, 1944. There were no survivors.

The Sloanes decided to build a memorial for their son and all others who lost their lives in World War II. Word of the project struck a responsive chord in the hearts of people throughout the world. Unusual stones and rare rocks poured in from every state in order that all of the United States might be represented in the shrine. In time, there were also more than one thousand unsolicited gifts of stones from ninety-one other nations.

Stones from all of the fifty states were used to shape the Altar of the Nation, which is mounted with a simple cross of New Hampshire granite. The cement used to make the altar was mixed with holy soil from Jerusalem.

A fieldstone lodge building was constructed for special indoor religious services. Its interior walls are faced with donated bits of stone and, behind glass prisms, such gifts as fragments of the bones of Saint Francis of Assisi and Saint Vincent de Paul.

Governors of every state and territory of the United States contributed, among others, to a sixty-eight-foot memorial bell tower dedicated to all American women who sacrificed their lives in the wars of the country.

The cathedral was dedicated in 1946. In the years since, thousands of services have been held at the cathedral by all denominations. The cathedral is open without charge from May to November for prayer and meditation.

Before his death in December, 1972, Dr. Sloan was very much in evidence at Halo Hill during the summer months. "The cathedral," he said in the summer before his death, "was the plan or creation of God. He used me to begin it."

The cathedral with its tall pines and its almost mystical hush inspires a religious awe. People indeed come here to meditate and, when emotions are kindled, many of them weep.

It was for this reason, Dr. Sloane said, he added two small chapels, the Chapel of Saint Francis of Assisi and the Mother's Chapel along the crest of the knoll. They are designed as places where a visitor might be by himself for meditation. Both are garden areas.

On the slope behind both altars, there are plantings of azaleas, mountain laurel and rhododendron. There are also roses, wide borders of annuals and stands of purple lilac, New Hampshire's state flower. And towering above them all are the cathedral pines.

The cemetery that gardeners and tourists visit for its outstanding displays of plant material is *Swan Point Cemetery* in Providence, Rhode Island.

Swan Point was started in 1847 and, from the beginning, its rolling hills and tree-covered landscape have been planted and maintained in a park-like manner. Over the years a number of more or less exotic plants have been introduced to complement the natural plant material, and the cemetery has become somewhat of a classroom for a number of schools and colleges where landscape architecture and horticulture are being taught.

Greenhouses have been maintained on the grounds since almost the beginning. Flower beds of annuals and perennials are used to enhance the beauty of the landscape. And a tulip festival is held in early May, followed by a hardy chrysanthemum show in mid-October.

Swan Point's list of trees and shrubs pinpoints 61 species and varieties of deciduous shrubs, including azaleas, deutzia, hydrangeas and viburnum. There are 94 varieties of deciduous trees, 43 varieties of evergreen shrubs, and 60 varieties of evergreen trees.

CHAPTER 8
A LISTING OF
OPEN GARDENS

Following is a list of open gardens by state and community. The hours, of course, are subject to change. In some cases, the gardens which are a part of house museums may be visited free, while there is an admission charge to the houses.

CONNECTICUT

State flower, mountain laurel. State tree, white oak.

BRISTOL

Chrysanthemum Festival, first two weeks in October. This city, where much pioneer work in the development and crossbreeding of the chrysanthemum was done at the Bristol Nurseries, is sometimes known as Mum City. The chrysanthemum provides the background for an annual festival, featuring activities in the arts and athletics.

FAIRFIELD

Birdcraft Sanctuary-Museum, 314 Unquowa Road, five acres with nature trails. See Chapter 3.

Roy and Margot Larsen Audubon Sanctuary, 2325 Burr Street, one hundred fifty acres with trails and "Singing and Fragrance Walk for the Blind." See Chapter 3.

Dogwood Festival in the Fairfield village of Greenfield Hill, two weeks in early May. More than thirty-thousand flaming dogwood trees around village green and areas beyond. Home and garden tours, special events, flower stalls. See Chapter 1.

FARMINGTON

Shade Swamp Sanctuary, off Route 6, a mile west of its intersection with Route 10, eight hundred acres, state-owned and managed by

State Board of Fisheries and Game, has marked trails leading to points of botanical interest. Wild flowers.

GRANBY, SIMSBURY, AND CANTON

McLean Game Refuge, thirty-four hundred acres, privately maintained sanctuary established by the late George P. McLean, one-time Governor and United States Senator. Motor trails and hiking trails with some trees and plants labeled. A large part is left as natural as possible to be a natural laboratory for the study of forestry, ecology, botany and conservation. Main entrance for auto drive on Route 10 between Simbury and Granby.

GREENWICH

The Audubon Center of Greenwich, 613 Riversville Road, 461 acres, includes the former Fairchild Connecticut Garden. Self-guiding nature trails, interpretive building with exhibits. Open all year Tuesday through Saturday. See Chapter 3.

GREENWICH, COS COB SECTION

Montgomery Pinetum, Bible Street. Open to residents of Greenwich only. Woodland area where the late Colonel Robert H. Montgomery developed a collection of conifers on sixty acres was bequeathed by him to Greenwich in 1953 to be preserved as a public park or garden. Small ponds, trails, winding brook banked by masses of primula japonica. *Greenwich Garden Center*, located here, plants thousands of tulips and daffodils in the area.

GUILFORD

Henry Whitfield House (1639), Whitfield Street. The house of the founder of Guilford has an extensive herb garden. Small admission charge to the house, where a list and description

HENRY WHITEFIELD HOUSE, GUILFORD, CONNECTICUT

of the herbs are available. A State Historical Museum. Garden free. Museum open Tuesdays through Sundays, except from December 15 to January 15.

HARTFORD

Elizabeth Park, Prospect and Asylum Avenues, one hundred acres with world-famous rose garden. Three-acre garden has more than fourteen thousand roses in some eleven hundred varieties. Annual, perennial and rock gardens. Spring flower show a week before Easter, chrysanthemum show in October. See Chapter 7.

Harriet Beecher Stowe House (1871), 77 Forest Street, maintained by the Stowe-Day Foundation. Grounds are a part of Nook Farm, which includes the *Mark Twain House* (1873–1874). The Stowe garden of old-fashioned flowers has been carefully re-created. Grounds free, admission to house. See Chapter 4.

LITCHFIELD

Tapping Reeve House (1773) *and Law School* (1784), South Street, maintained by Litchfield Historical Society. Small formal garden of geometric pattern with brick walks around round beds. Planted with seasonal flowers, tulips in spring, annuals during summer, and chrysanthemums in fall. Bordering beds with perennials and lilies. Admission to house.

White Flower Farm, on Route 63, former farm now a nursery and commercial greenhouses operated by Mr. and Mrs. William Harris. One greenhouse with tuberous begonias. One garden contains plants from the Gotelli Dwarf Evergreen Collection, all grown from cuttings taken at the National Arboretum in Washington, D.C. Extensive garden center open daily from April to October, weekends during winter.

White Memorial Foundation, Bissell Road off Route 25, Litchfield Nature Center and Museum, four thousand acres in Litchfield and Morris. Nature trail where the blind can "feel" nature, wild flowers, extensive trails. See Chapter 3.

MYSTIC

Mystic Seaport, Greenmanville Avenue, a recreated nineteenth century New England coastal village with forty buildings on thirty-seven acres, impressive whaleships, schooners and other vessels recalling the age of sail. Gardens include contemporary examples of plants at Mystic Seaport Stores, marigolds, cosmos, petunias and begonias; Buckingham House herb garden outside of kitchen wing of house built in 1768; typical vegetable garden at the *Edwards House* (circa 1805), the home of a seagoing man and his family.

Pequot-Sepos Wildlife Sanctuary, Pequot-sepos Road, a hundred twenty-five acres plus ninety-three in Stonington. Nature trails with more than one hundred fifty different plant species labeled, a special fern trail with descriptions of their life cycle. Exhibits at the *Trailside Natural History and Conservation Museum*.

Museum open daily except Mondays.

NEW HAVEN

East Rock Park, Orange Street. Municipal park, dating from 1880, with picnic grounds and hiking trails, covers 446 acres. The park embraces the *Pardee Rose Gardens*, a six-acre garden built in the early 1920s on the eastern side of East Rock Park. Spring, fall and Christmas flower shows at the Pardee Greenhouses nearby. See Chapter 7.

West Rock Nature Center, in West Rock Park, Wintergreen Avenue, fifty acres with a nature trail and zoo. See Chapter 7.

Yale University campus, with daily tours from Visitors Center, Phelps Gateway, College Street. The thousand-acre campus has fine specimen trees, large mass plantings of rhododendron and laurel, espaliered wisteria on buildings. Borders in courtyards have English ivy as ground cover, with thousands of daffodils naturalized in the ground cover to provide a spectacular display in the spring. Noteworthy is the *Sterling Divinity Quadrangle*, Prospect Street, a part of the Yale University Divinity School. A central mall, with a row of elms down the center, has plantings of laurel and dogwood. Six small courtyards around the mall have plantings of small flowering trees and mass plantings of evergreens and rhododendron. The university owns the *Yale Natural Preserve*, along the west side of *Ray Tomkins Memorial*, two hundred acres of wooded land with a wild flower and bird sanctuary.

Edgerton Gardens, Whitney Avenue, the former twenty-five acre Brewster Estate being developed as an arboretum by the city. See Chapter 7.

Pardee-Morris House (1780), 325 Lighthouse Road. Small herb garden. Open May to November, except Sundays. Donation to house.

NEW LONDON

Connecticut Arboretum at Connecticut College, Williams Street. More than four hundred species and varieties of trees and shrubs on three hundred fifty acres. Mountain laurel best seen in mid-June. Also the *Caroline Black Botanical Garden* with an attractive display of ornamental trees and shrubs. See Chapter 2.

NORTH COVENTRY

Caprilands Herb Farm, Silver Street. Extensive herb gardens on fifty-acre farm with eighteenth century house. Visitors may sample the gourmet cooking and tour the gardens of Mrs. Adelma Grenier Simmons, garden writer. Gardens illustrate the history and uses of herbs from medieval times to present. Open April to December.

NORWICH

Memorial Rose Garden in Mohegan Park, two acres with more than three thousand bushes of one hundred seventy-five varieties. See Chapter 7.

SHARON

Sharon Audubon Center, on Route 4, two miles southeast of Sharon, 526-acre wildlife sanctuary with trails and herb garden, operated by the National Audubon Center. See Chapter 1.

STAMFORD

The Bartlett Arboretum, Brookdale Road, sixty-two acres operated by the University of Connecticut's College of Agriculture and Natural Resources, walks and nature trails. Nearby at 39 Scofieldtown Road is Stamford Museum and Nature Center with nature trails. See Chapter 2.

STORRS

The University of Connecticut at Storrs, Floriculture Display and Trial Gardens, Route 195. Perennial borders, trial beds for annuals, collections of herbs, taxus and dwarf trees. See Chapter 2.

STRATFORD

Boothe Memorial Park, Main Street. Trial garden for roses, peonies, iris, gladiolus. Maintained by the town. Free.

Sterling House Community Center and Park, 2283 Main Street. Grounds of more than three acres include a garden designed by Charles Downing Lay, landscape architect, and maintained by part-time help and volunteers. Garden framed by towering cryptomeria trees, with center mall bordered by holly trees and hawthorn. Bloom is best in spring when flowering trees, peonies and iris are in flower.

TORRINGTON

Laurel Mountain, Mountain Road off Route 4, in foothills of the Berkshires includes some one hundred acres acquired during the past twenty-five years by Paul Freedman, conservation specialist. He designed and enlarged laurel groves to cover thirty-six acres with marked trails and initiated a Laurel Festival. The cascading masses of that state flower now draw as many as twenty-five thousand visitors during their bloom in June.

VOLUNTOWN, NORTH STONINGTON, GRISWOLD AND OTHER TOWNS.

Pachaug Forest, Ranger Headquarters off Route 49, mile north of intersection with Route 138. 22,389 acres, with hiking trails, a nursery for tree seedlings, two large stands of rhododendrons, wild flowers in the largest of the state's forests.

WATERBURY

Hamilton Park, Plank Road and Silver Street, rose garden of 14,400 square feet with two thousand varieties of roses, annual flower beds in different areas. See Chapter 7.

WATERFORD

Harkness Memorial State Park, 275 Great Neck Road. Former 235-acre estate of Mr. and Mrs. Edward Stephens Harkness, with forty-two room mansion. Extensive formal gardens with exotic plants, topiary, roses, rare trees. Also greenhouses with exotic specimens. Open May to October. Admission. See Chapter 6.

WESTPORT

Mid-Fairfield County Youth Museum, 10 Woodside Lane. Live animals, exhibits, nature trails. Free.

WOODBURY

Flanders Nature Center, Church Hill Road, one hundred thirty acres with three miles of trails named for interest, such as botany, plant succession, geology. Self-guiding leaflets pinpoint such points of interest as azaleas and a nut tree arboretum. The land, once part of Van Vleck Farm, is owned by Miss Natalie Van Vleck who wanted the land to be used for passive recreation. The *Flanders Nature Center, Inc.*, was formed in 1963 to operate the leased land and preserve it as a natural area. Open daily.

WOODSTOCK

Bowen House (*Roseland Cottage*), on Route 169, formal garden in estate layout of the nineteenth century. Owned by the Society for the Preservation of New England Antiquities, which hopes to put it in better condition at some time.

MAINE

State flower, pine cone and tassel. State tree, Eastern white pine.

AUGUSTA

Blaine House (State Executive Mansion), State Street. Former home of James Blaine, who was defeated for the Presidency in 1884. Three-acre gardens and grounds with formal garden, private garden, shrub borders. See Chapter 6.

BAR HARBOR

Acadia National Park, headquarters at Hulls Cove, occupying nearly half of Mount Desert Island, is a wildlife sanctuary with scores of varieties of wild flowers, a hundred miles of trails. A wild flower garden at *Sieur de Mont's Spring* is a project of the Bar Harbor Garden Club.

CALAIS

Moosehorn National Wildlife Refuge, four miles north of town on US 1. Aquarium, wildlife displays, auto tours, nature trails. Open June 15 to Labor Day. Free.

CAMDEN

Bok Amphitheater, Atlantic Avenue, behind the Camden Public Library, native trees, shrubs, plants about a horseshoe-shaped amphitheater, reminiscent of a Roman arena. See Chapter 1.

Merry Gardens, Simonton Road. Commercial greenhouses and formal herb gardens on half an acre. More than a thousand varieties of house plants and herbs. Open all year except Sundays.

CARIBOU

Nylander Museum, 393 Main Street. Town museum named after its founder, Olaf Nylander (1864–1943), as a tribute to a self-taught scientist who compiled data on local geology, flora, marine life and shells. Museum has seasonal and regular exhibits of woody plants, orchids of Maine, leaves of native trees, wild flowers. Open Monday through Friday. Free.

DEER ISLE

Ames Pond, on Route 15 in Stonington. Pink and white water lilies in bloom late June to early September.

ELLSWORTH

John Black Mansion (1802), West Main Street. Formal garden at rear of Georgian mansion enclosed by a lilac hedge. Open June to November, gardens free.

Stanwood Museum and Bird Sanctuary, Bar Harbor Road, a fifty-acre wildlife preserve with many nature trails. House, which was birthplace of pioneer ornithologist, Cordelia J. Stanwood, is maintained as museum. Open daily mid-June to mid-September. Donations welcome.

FREEPORT

Mast Landing Sanctuary, Mast Landing Road, self-guiding trails on fifteen hundred acres, maintained by the Maine Audubon Society. Open daily. Donations. See Chapter 3.

GEORGETOWN

The Josephine H. Newman Sanctuary, Small Road between east and west branches of Robinhood Cove, four hundred acres owned by the Maine Audubon Society. Many trails with wild flowers on land left to the society by Mrs. Newman, a distinguished amateur naturalist. Open daily.

LEWISTON

Thorncrag Sanctuary, Montello Street. Several man-made ponds, nature trails on two hundred twenty-six acres owned by the Stanton Bird Club. Open all year. Free.

NORTHEAST HARBOR

Thuya Gardens, on Asticou Terraces. Simple flower borders, free-form pool and Alberta spruces on land donated to the town by Joseph Curtis, landscape architect.

ORONO

Fay Hyland Botanical Plantation at the University of Maine, College Avenue. Three acres with more than three hundred species of trees and shrubs, many species of ferns and flowering plants. Open all year. Free.

PORTLAND

Deering Oaks, Deering and Forest avenues, fifty-three acre park with eighteen-bed *Rose Circle*, seven hundred roses, other beds of annuals, perennials. See Chapter 7.

Wadsworth-Longfellow House (1785), 487 Congress Street. Former home of poet Henry Wadsworth Longfellow with long and well-maintained garden, much as Longfellow knew it. Open mid-May to mid-October, daily except Sunday. Admission. See Chapter 4.

PRESQUE ISLAND

Aroostook Experimental Farm, Houlton Road. Some three hundred seventy-five acres operated by the University of Maine for experiments in improving potato and sugar beet growing. Guided service weekdays. Free.

ROCKLAND

Private sunken garden at the home of Mr. and Mrs. Eugene W. Ureneff, 169 Camden Street. Begun in 1962 and open to the public in summer months until 5 P.M. Garden, in a wild natural setting with a brook running through the center, has forty-eight of the standard type and fourteen hanging tuberous begonia plants, a profusion of ferns and wild flowers.

ROCKPORT

Children's Chapel, Calderwood Lane on Beauchamp Point. Open chapel building overlooking the sea. Nicely landscaped grounds include a herb garden, extensive planting of roses, annuals, perennials. See Chapter 1.

SOUTH BERWICK

Hamilton House (1785), Route 236. Formal garden with terraces and statuary, created by the Society for the Preservation of New England Antiquities in the context of an estate layout at the turn of the century. Open mid-June to mid-September, Wednesday through Saturday 1 to 5. Admission.

Sarah Orne Jewett Memorial (1774), Route 236. Birthplace of novelist, maintained by the Society for the Preservation of New England Antiquities. Small formal garden. Open mid-June to mid-September, Wednesday through Saturday, 1 to 5. Admission.

SOUTH HARPSWELL

Private garden of Dr. and Mrs. Currier McEwen, Route 123, open by written or telephone appointment only. The couple specialize in Siberian and Japanese irises and daylilies and plant about one thousand Siberian seedlings each year, an equal number of daylilies, and about three hundred Japanese iris. The garden consists of three quarters of an acre. The Siberian irises are in bloom from mid-June to early July, the Japanese irises through July, and the daylilies are in bloom from late June to mid-August.

SPRINGVALE

Harvey Butler Rhododendron Sanctuary, two miles from center on Oak Street. This largest and northernmost stand of the great laurel or rosebay in the country is a property of the New England Wild Flower Society, Inc.

STANDISH

Daniel Marrett House (1789), on Route 25. House museum, maintained by the Society for the Preservation of New England Antiquities, has small formal garden. Open Sunday and Monday, 1 to 5, July 1 to mid-September. Admission.

STONINGTON (See Deer Isle)

VINALHAVEN

Ambrust Hill Reservation, Atlantic Avenue, wildlife sanctuary on Vinalhaven Island, owned by the town and planted by the Vinalhaven Garden Club. See Chapter 3.

WISCASSET

Nickels-Sortwell House (1807), Main Street. Federal mansion, maintained by the Society for the Preservation of New England Antiquities, has enclosed town garden with border plantings. Open Tuesday through Saturday, 11 to 5, and Sunday, 2 to 5, mid-June to mid-October. Admission. See Chapter 1.

Sunken garden on Main Street, located within a former house foundation, maintained by the town. Small beds and borders with annuals and perennials. See Chapter 1.

WOOLWICH

Robert P. Tristram Coffin Wild Flower Reservation, on Merrimeeting Bay, a property of the New England Wild Flower Society, Inc. A tract of one hundred seventy-five acres, including woods, fields, brooks and tidal marsh, with ferns and wild flowers.

MASSACHUSETTS

State flower, may flower. State tree, American elm.

ANDOVER

Rhododendron Garden, established about 1875, on campus of the University of Massachusetts, Route 116. Azaleas in bloom May 15–June 10, rhododendrons late May, and mountain laurel late May to mid-June. Also, fine examples of Sciadopitys verticillata.

ANDOVER

Amos Blanchard House (1819), 97 Main Street, owned by the Andover Historical Society. Border garden maintained by the Andover Garden Club.

Phillips Academy Bird Sanctuary, Chapel Avenue. Sanctuary owned by Phillips Academy is most noteworthy in May and early June when azaleas and rhododendrons are in bloom.

ARLINGTON

Jason Russell House, circa 1680, 7 Jason Street. Garden maintained by the Arlington Garden Club.

ASHLEY FALLS

Bartholomew's Cobble, mile west of traffic light in town center. A one hundred seventy-four-acre property of The Trustees of Reservations, famed for its wild flowers and plants, waterfowl, marsh and song birds. Portions border Weatogue Road and Andrus Road. Within the reservation is the *Ashley House*, built in 1735, the oldest dwelling in western Massachusetts. Open April 15 to October 15. Admission.

BARRE

Cook's Canyon, South Street. Thirty-five acres with nature trails, dramatic gorge. A bequest of Mrs. Mary L. Cook to the Massa-

chusetts Audubon Society.

BOSTON

Arnold Arboretum, at junction of Routes 1 and 28, administered by Harvard University with the cooperation of the Boston Department of Parks and Recreation, has been called America's greatest garden. Established in 1872, its two hundred and sixty-five acres contain some six thousand varieties or ornamental trees and shrubs. See Chapter 2.

The Fenway Gardens, Boylston Street and Park Drive, some three hundred individual flower and vegetable gardens, on seven acres, planted by members of the Fenway Garden Society. The gardens are an outgrowth of the Victory Gardens of World War II.

Fenway Rose Garden, The Fenway, Park Drive, in the vicinity of the Boston Museum of Fine Arts, two-acre rose garden with labeled specimens, maintained by the Parks Department, thousands of roses in formal beds.

Isabella Stewart Gardner Museum, 280 The Fenway. A mansion, in the architectural style of Venetian palaces of the XV–XVI centuries, was dismantled in part in Venice and brought to Boston by Mrs. Gardner, and rebuilt, with galleries open to an immense court. Museum greenhouses furnish rare and exotic plants. The court, with its pillars, arches, statuary and ancient columns, is open to a height of four stories and enclosed by a glassed-in roof. Plantings may include such things as hydrangeas in pots, orchids, begonias and ground covers. A walled outer garden has rhododendrons, other plantings, and is open at intervals during the growing season. Museum, open all year, is closed Mondays and holidays September through

THE GARDENS AT BOSTON'S ISABELLA STEWART GARDNER MUSEUM

June, closed Sunday and Monday during July and August. Free.

Mother Church Park, First Church of Christ, Scientist, Massachusetts Avenue and Huntington Avenue, seven acres of landscaping and flower beds in the new Christian Science Center complex. See Chapter 7.

Public Garden, Charles Street, twenty-four-acre gardens with three-acre pond, created 1859. Outstanding specimens of Sophora japonica. Flowers in huge beds throughout the gardens change with the seasons. See Chapter 7.

Suffolk County Courthouse, Pemberton Square, near Government Center, and behind Center Plaza, rooftop garden created by John E. Powers, clerk of the Supreme Judicial Court. Open only by appointment. See Chapter 7.

BOURNE

Aptucxet Trading Post, 24 Aptucxet Road, replica of 1627 trading post with small, square herb garden planted by members of the Aptucxet Garden Club. Open April to November. Admission.

BRAINTREE

Sylvanus Thayer House (1720), 786 Washington Street. A period garden designed by the Braintree Garden Club. Flowers, shrubs, herb gardens. Open mid-April to mid-October, Tuesday, Thursday, Friday, Sunday 1:30 to 4, Saturday from 10:30. Admission. See Chapter 4.

BREWSTER

Cape Cod Museum of Natural History, Route 6A. Exhibition pavilion and nature trails. Open daily all year. Admission.

Cape Cod National Seashore, some forty-four hundred acres with visitor centers at Eastham and Provincetown. Bicycle trails well developed in Province Lands and Pilgrim Heights. A trail for the blind at Salt Pond in Eastham. Beaches in Eastham, South Wellfleet, Truro, and Provincetown. See Chapter 1.

CAMBRIDGE

Harvard Botanical Museum, Oxford Street, the Ware Collection of Blaschka glass models of plants. More than three thousand models, 874 different species. See Chapter 5.

Mt. Auburn Cemetery, 580 Mt. Auburn Street. Some sixteen hundred labeled trees on one hundred sixty-five acres in the first "garden cemetery" in America. Founded in 1831, it started a trend which became well established by the twentieth century. Trees, imported from many countries, include Oriental flowering crabapples, Japanese cherries, magnolias, Turkish hazel, and Japanese cork.

CHELMSFORD

Barrett-Byam Homestead Museum, Byam Road. Museum, maintained by the Chelmsford Historical Society, has flower borders and herb garden planted as a joint project of five garden clubs.

Bartlett Park, Acton Road, three and one half acres in the town center given to the town's Land Conservation Trust early in 1961 by Miss Harriett Bartlett. The trust, with the aid of an Arnold Arboretum staff member, set up an arboretum of more than two hundred trees and shrubs, including flowering crabs, conifers, birches, larch, dogwoods, and stands of azaleas, rhododendron and mountain laurel.

CONCORD

Great Meadows National Wildlife Refuge, headquarters on Sudbury Road. Sanctuary, including section in Sudbury, will total four thousand acres when complete. Nature trails, bicycle paths. Open all year.

Old Manse (1769), Monument Street at the Old North Bridge. One-time home of Ralph Waldo Emerson and Nathaniel Hawthorne has small herb garden, ancient lilacs and flower beds bordering a long grape arbor. Grounds free.

Orchard House (1650 with 1730 addition), 399 Lexington Road. Wild flower garden. Grounds free. See Chapter 6.

DANVERS

Glen Magna, Centre Street off U.S. Route 1, twenty-room mansion owned by Captain Joseph Peabody of Salem, sea merchant who made a fortune in the China trade. Estate, owned by the Danvers Historical Society, has an architecturally stunning teahouse, designed and carved by Samuel McIntire, Salem architect. The grounds consist of majestic lawns with a series of gardens, ancient trees, fountain and pool, and Etruscan urns. An English-type garden has crab and cherry trees, hedges of buckthorn and arborvitae, beds of peonies. A garden area with Chinese cherry trees includes a pagoda formed by Corinthian columns, which support huge wisteria vines. There is a brick walled rose garden with fountain by the teahouse. Open mid-May to mid-October, 10 to 4. Admission.

DENNIS

Jericho, Trotting Park Road, 1801 house and barn museum, maintained by the Dennis Historical Society. Flower gardens planted by the West Dennis Garden Club. Open Wednesday and Friday, 2 to 4, during summer months.

EASTHAMPTON

Arcadia, Clapp Street off Route 10, three hundred-acre sanctuary of the Massachusetts Audubon Society, bordering Connecticut River. Swamp and uplands with berry-bearing trees and shrubs and a hummingbird garden.

FALMOUTH

Ashumet Holly Reservation, north side of Route 151 in East Falmouth, forty-five acres, Massachusetts Audubon Society. Famous for the number and varieties of American holly trees. Guided walks, annual holly sale, trails.

Julia Wood House (1790), 55 Palmer Avenue. Colonial garden maintained by the Falmouth Garden Club. Open June 15 to Sept. 15, 2 to 5. Admission to house, grounds free.

FRAMINGHAM

Garden in the Woods, Hemenway Road, forty-three-acre tract with more than four thousand species and varieties of native American wild flowers along five miles of trails. Headquarters of the New England Wild Flower Society, Inc. See Chapter 3.

GLOUCESTER

Eastern Point, Eastern Point Boulevard, twenty-six acres of marsh, woods and ocean headlands owned by the Massachusetts Audubon Society. In September and October, seaside goldenrods attract thousands of migrating monarch butterflies.

GRANVILLE

Phelon Hill, off Route 57, dramatic display of mountain laurel in mid-June. Other displays of the pink and white laurel in *Granville State Forest*.

GREAT BARRINGTON

Laurel Festival, sponsored ʀʏ the Chamber of Commerce, has special events, such as sidewalk art shows and parades, in the area towns during the weeks when laurel blossoms, about May 15 through June. Charted laurel trails of several miles southwest to Mount Washington on the Massachusetts–New York border.

HAMPDEN

Laughing Brook, 789 Main Street, sanctuary of two hundred fifty acres maintained by the Massachusetts Audubon Society. Heart of the sanctuary is the estate of Thornton Burgess, author of children's books. Museum nature center, wildlife trails, extensive programs for children. Open summer months, closed Mondays.

HANCOCK

Hancock Shaker Village, at junction of Routes 20 and 41, restored village where Shakers lived from 1790 to 1960. Shops, barns and houses on nine hundred thirty-five acres. Extensive herb garden with white fence bordering it, which is covered with rose gallica. The Shakers were the first people in this country to grow herbs on a large scale for the pharmaceutical market. The herb garden here is planted with material that constituted the major crops of the Hancock Shakers' dried herb and extract business. Open June to mid-October. Admission.

HINGHAM

Old Ordinary (1650), 19 Lincoln Street. Authentically furnished home maintained by the Hingham Historical Society has garden planted by the Garden Club of Hingham. Open mid-June to Labor Day, Tuesday through Saturday. Admission.

HINGHAM AND COHASSET

Whitney and Thayer Woods, on Route 3A opposite Sohier Street. Marked nature trails in seven hundred ninety-five acres of property of The Trustees of Reservations are noted for rhododendrons and azaleas.

HOPKINTON

Weston Nurseries, East Main Street. Largest commercial nursery in the east on five hundred acres specializes on plant life that is hardy in that area. Landscaped garden in the Japanese-American style has paths, pools, pruned evergreens and perennial beds. Experimental gardens in the summer months. Open all year, except Sundays.

IPSWICH

The John Whipple House (1640), 53 South Main Street. House, restored and furnished by the Ipswich Historical Society. An outstanding herb garden designed by Arthur A. Shurcliff. Open mid-April to October, daily except Monday. Admission. See Chapter 4.

Thomas F. Waters Memorial (1795), opposite Whipple House. Property of the Ipswich Historical Society has formal garden in courtyard. Open mid-April to October, daily except Monday. Admission.

LENOX

Pleasant Valley, eastern slope of Lenox Mountain, Clifford Street, six hundred sixty acres of natural wilderness in Berkshire Hills, maintained by the Massachusetts Audubon Society. House, barns and acreage of Revolutionary period farm, trailside museum, eleven miles of nature trails.

Tanglewood, West Street. Famed for the annual Tanglewood Music Festival with concerts by the Boston Symphony Orchestra. The two hundred ten acre grounds, developed into a gentleman's estate by William Aspinwall Tappan, were given to the Boston Symphony by Mrs. Gorham Brooks and Miss Mary Aspinwall Tappan in 1936. Extensive lawns with distant views of the Berkshires, hemlock gardens with manicured hedges, tall pines. Grounds free, daily except during festival.

LEXINGTON

Lexington Gardens, 93 Hancock Street. Commercial nursery on ten acres with greenhouses has hundreds of varieties of potted plants, roses, annuals in season. An indoor garden is landscaped around a waterfall, a water wheel and bonsai. Lectures are given weekly in the fall. Open all year except Sundays.

LINCOLN

Codman House, Route 117, South Great Road. A nineteenth and early twentieth century estate with formal gardens, including pool and statuary, being restored by the Society for the Preservation of New England Antiquities. Admission.

Drumlin Farm, a National Environmental Education Landmark, South Great Road, headquarters of the Massachusetts Audubon Society, two hundred twenty acres with self-guiding trails, live exhibits of domestic and wild animals, vegetable garden, herb garden. Admission.

LONGMEADOW

The Fannie Stebbins Memorial Wildlife Refuge, Meadow Road. A three hundred twenty-acre sanctuary maintained by the Fannie Stebbins Memorial Wildlife Refuge, Inc., in Longmeadow Flats near the Connecticut River. Self-guiding nature trails.

MARBLEHEAD

King Hooper Mansion (1728), 8 Hooper Street, headquarters of the Marblehead Arts Association. Garden, restored by the Arrangers of Marblehead, has beds with boxwood borders, annuals, perennials, small kitchen herb garden, flowering shurbs. Admission to house, garden free. See Chapter 4.

MASHPEE

Lowell Holly Reservation, South Sandwich Road. A peninsula of one hundred thirty acres bordered by Wakeby Pond, property of The Trustees of Reservations, features American holly, beech trees, laurel and rhododendron.

MEDFIELD

Medfield Rhododendron Reservation, off Route 27 opposite Kingsbury Pond. A property of The Trustees of Reservations, consisting of one hundred ninety acres with trails and paths.

MILTON

Blue Hills Trailside Museum, Route 138, Canton Avenue, six thousand-acre sanctuary operated by the Boston Zoological Society for the Metropolitan District Commission, with nature trails, woodland garden, plant specimens under glass in museum. See Chapter 3.

Rocky Knoll Nature Center, 74 Maple Street, two acres of oak trees and a center for teaching conservation in an urban community. Maintained by the Massachusetts Audubon Society.

MONSON

Tupper Hill, Peck Road off Monson-Wales Road, three thousand acre sanctuary established by Arthur D. Norcross includes bogs, engineered lakes, brooks, waterfalls. Motor tours by appointment daily except Sundays and holidays, by appointment. See Chapter 3.

NORFOLK

Stony Brook Nature Center, near junction of North, Pond and Needham streets, off Route 115, operated by Massachusetts Audubon Society in conjunction with two hundred-acre Bristol-Blake State Reservation. Self-guiding nature trails border swamps and ponds.

NORTHAMPTON

Botanic Garden, Smith College, three hundred-acre campus designed as an arboretum, with extensive gardens, greenhouses, flower shows. Open all year, free. See Chapter 2.

NORTH ANDOVER

Stevens-Coolidge Place, 138 Andover Street, house in colonial revival style has extensive gardens on eighty-nine acres. Maintained by The Trustees of Reservations. Mixed hardwood trees, exotic plants, perennial borders, sunken garden with statuary. Gardens open mid-May to mid-October without charge. See Chapter 6.

PAXTON

Moore State Park, two miles from center, off Route 31. Former Josiah A. Spaulding estate with pond, brook, waterfall. Noted for rhododendrons, spring flowers and fall foliage.

PERU

Dorothy Frances Rice Sanctuary, South Road. Wildlife sanctuary established as memorial has blazed nature trails, visitors' center for nature study groups. Open summers except on Tuesdays. Register at center before using trails. Free.

PETERSHAM

Fisher Museum, Harvard Forest, Route 32, three miles north of center. Historical and silvicultural dioramas and case exhibits, depicting history of New England land use, methods of silviculture (forest management), methods of pruning and weeding. A part of Harvard University. Nature tracts. Open Monday through Saturday, 9 to 5, Sunday 2 to 5. Free.

Rutland Brook, on Connor Pond off Route 122. Hilly sanctuary of one hundred ten acres, owned by the Massachusetts Audubon Society, is named for the stream which runs through it. It has majestic hemlocks and, in spring, many ferns and wild flowers along the trail.

PHILLIPSTON

Elliott Laurel Reservation, on Route 101, a quarter mile west of public beach at Queen Lake. Half mile nature trail on twenty-five-acre reservation, owned by The Trustees of Reservations. Stands of laurel usually in bloom third week of June.

PITTSFIELD

Springside Park Gardens, 874 North Street, 231-acre municipal park, with rose gardens of three beds with about fifty roses each. Flower gardens consist primarily of a colorful display of seven thousand tulips in the spring, followed by some five thousand annuals.

PLYMOUTH

Plimoth Plantation, three miles south on Route 3A, re-creation of original Plymouth Colony as it was in 1627. Each house in the village has its own herb garden. Open April to November. Admission. See Chapter 4.

PRINCETON

Wachusett Meadows, Goodnow Road, 750 acres with mountain upland of forest and meadow, nature trails include a maple swamp with boardwalk. Property of Massachusetts Audubon Society.

QUINCY

Adams National Historic Site, 135 Adams Street. Former estate of the John Adams family with five acres close to the heart of a busy and crowded city. Old trees, extensive old-fashioned flower gardens. Open late April to November. Admission. See Chapter 4.

READING

Parker Tavern (1694), 103 Washington Street. Home maintained by the Reading Antiquarian Society with kitchen garden planted by the Reading Garden Club after careful research. Open May to November, Sundays 2 to 5, other times by appointment.

SALEM

Essex Institute, 132 Essex Street. This giant county historical society consists of a museum and library, five house museums, and two other buildings with period exhibits. Its historic houses, some a little distance from the museum complex, include fine examples of the design and carvings of Samuel McIntire, Salem architect. Gardens at the various houses are representative of the seventeenth, eighteenth and nineteenth centuries. On the museum grounds is a boxwood garden laid out in the eighteenth-century style, featuring several kinds of boxwood, magnolias, roses and lilies. The *John Ward House* (1684) has a herb garden. Other houses with period gardens: the *Crowinshield-Bentley House* (1727), the *Gardner-Pingree House* (1804), the *Peirce-Nichols House* (1782), and the *Assembly House* (1782). The museum is open free all year. Houses are open during summer months Tuesday through Saturday. Admission.

The First Church Garden, 316 Essex Street. One of the oldest continuous gardens in the

United States, begun in the seventeenth century. Memorial arbor, rhododendrons, shrubs, seasonal flowers. See Chapter 1.

House of Seven Gables (1668), 54 Turner Street. House, built by mariner John Turner close to the sea's edge, was made famous by Nathaniel Hawthorne's novel. Three other houses were moved to the site to form a complex of historic buildings. These are the *Hathaway House* (1682), the *Retire Becket House* (1655), and the *Birthplace of Nathaniel Hawthorne* (circa 1750). The houses form a court with a lawn and charming gardens. One small garden is filled with plants mentioned by Hawthorne, among them feverfew, balsam, coxcomb and salpiglossis. A rose garden is brightened by the white Scotch rose. A herb garden has plants for hearth cooking and the preservation of food. Open all year. Admission.

Peabody Museum, 161 Essex Street. Famed maritime museum in old East India Marine Hall has an Oriental-type garden with a crushed stone base and a large bronze temple garden lantern. Trees and shrubs which grow in Japan or China range from locusts and hemlocks to golden rain tree and azaleas. Open all year. Admission.

Ropes Mansion (1719) 318 Essex Street. Formal period garden with pool, large beds forming two concentric circles about a sundial, crosswalks, and rectangular beds in other areas. Shrubs, perennials and annuals, many of them grown in the greenhouse adjacent to the mansion. Open May to October. No charge for gardens.

SANDWICH

Heritage Plantation, Grove and Pine Streets. Outstanding museum of Americana, dedicated to the memory of Josiah Kirby Lilly Jr., distinguished collector of Americana. Has extensive plantings of rhododendron on its seventy-six acres, specimen trees, shrubs, flowers. Open early June to late October. Admission. See Chapter 5.

SCITUATE

Cudworth House (1797), First Parish Road, property of Scituate Historical Society. Small herb garden. Open June 15–September 15, Wednesday through Saturday, 2 to 5. Admission.

SHARON

Moose Hill, Moose Hill Street, off Route 27, oldest wildlife sanctuary of the Massachusetts Audubon Society, with three hundred ten acres of woodland. Wild flowers and fern garden.

SHELBURNE FALLS

Bridge of Flowers, on Route 2 along Mohawk Trail. Bridge, built in 1908 to carry trolley tracks across the Deerfield River, was abandoned in 1928 and converted from an eyesore into a pathway of flowers as a community project.

SHERBORN

Little Pond, South Street, four hundred twenty-seven acres of woodland and marsh trails. Massachusetts Audubon Society.

SPRINGFIELD

Edgewood Gardens on campus of American International College. Extensive beds of annuals with more than twenty-six thousand plants. See Chapter 1.

Forest Park, off Route 5. Municipal park of seven hundred sixty-five acres with half acre of rose beds, large annual garden, and greenhouse with exotic and traditional plants.

Storrowton, 1511 Memorial Avenue. A group of reconstructed old New England buildings around a village green. Herb garden, flower borders around some buildings. Open mid-June to Labor Day. Admission.

STOCKBRIDGE

Berkshire Garden Center, Larrywaug Corner. Eight acres operated as botanical garden. Rose garden, herb garden, daffodil bank, lily pond and greenhouses in scenic setting. See Chapter 1.

Naumkeag (*Choate Estate*), Prospect Hill Road. House of Joseph Choate, Ambassador to the Court of St. James's, was designed and built by architect Stanford White in 1885. A property of The Trustees of Reservations. Gardens were the creation of Mabel Choate. Promenades, fountains, terraces, Chinese garden. Open daily except Monday during summer. Admission.

STURBRIDGE VILLAGE, STURBRIDGE, MASSACHUSETTS

See Chapter 6.

Chesterwood, Route 183. Studio of Daniel Chester French, famed sculptor, with gardens and nature trails. Open mid-June to Labor Day. Admission. See Chapter 1.

Mission House (1739), Main Street. Home of the Reverend John Sergeant, missionary to the Indians, is now a museum of colonial life. A property of The Trustees of Reservations. Open June to October, except Mondays. Admission. See Chapter 4.

STURBRIDGE

Old Sturbridge Village, Route 20, one and one-half miles west of junction with Route 15. A recreation of a New England community reflecting American life in the period from 1790 to 1840. Herb gardens, formal gardens, orchards, farm garden. Open all year. Admission. See Chapter 4.

TOPSFIELD

Ipswich River Wildlife Sanctuary, Perkins Row. Largest sanctuary of the Massachusetts Audubon Society, with twenty-five hundred acres of marsh and upland. Many varieties of trees and shrubs place it among New England's larger arboretums, although they are not labeled and maintained.

WALTHAM

Gore Place (1805), Main and Gore streets. Country home of Governor Christopher Gore, a federal mansion with twenty-two rooms. The forty-five acre grounds include a herb garden, cutting garden and grape arbor. Arborvitae forms a circular screen around the cutting garden of rose trees, peonies, iris. Apple trees have been planted to re-establish the old orchard. Open mid-April to mid-November. Closed Mondays. Admission.

The Suburban Experiment Station, University of Massachusetts, 240 Beaver Street. Trial flower beds on acre and a half with annuals from July 1, perennials from June, test beds of entries for All-America Selections.

The Vale, Theodore Lyman House (1793), Lyman Street. Fine grounds in layout of nineteenth century estate, old azaleas and rhododendrons, greenhouses with grapevines and camellia trees grown there for more than a century. Property of Society for the Preservation of New England Antiquities. Open July and August, Thursday through Saturday. Admission. See Chapter 6.

WELLESLEY

Alexandra Botanic Garden and Hunnewell Arboretum, on portion of five hundred-acre campus of Wellesley College, Central and Washington streets. Deciduous trees, shrubs and evergreens on twenty-four acres. Greenhouses with exotic plants. See Chapter 2.

WESTFIELD

Grandmother's Garden, Smith Avenue. Botanical garden with herbs and old planting gardens set up in 1934 as a memorial to Mrs. Mary Steiger. April through October. Free.

Stanley Park, Kensington Avenue. Trails and gardens in thirty-eight acres on a site where managers and dealers of Stanley Home Products, Inc., held meetings. The park began to grow with the gift of one thousand roses, was organized as a charitable corporation in 1949, now has trails, ponds and a carillon tower with two sets of carillon. Open May to October. Free.

WESTON

The Case Estates, 135 Wellesley Street. A part of the Arnold Arboretum in Jamaica Plain, its one hundred thirteen acres have a variety of gardens, test plots and demonstration areas. See Chapter 2.

Hubbard Trail, Dean Road. A twenty-two-acre sanctuary, owned by the New England Wild Flower Society, Inc., noted for its wild flowers.

WINCHENDON

Arbutus Sanctuary, West Street. A ninety-nine-acre tract, owned by the New England Wild Flower Society, Inc., noted for its varied habitat and rich plant material. The wilderness area is a special sanctuary for trailing arbutus.

WINCHESTER

Rocky Ledge Farm & Nursery, 242 Cambridge Street. Commercial gardens and greenhouses on twenty-five acres includes an extensive American tea garden with teahouse, large boulders, exotic plants, white pines, fountain, small cascading waterfall. Some quarter million square feet of greenhouses with house plants, exotic plants. Open all year except Sundays.

WORCESTER

Rose quadrangle on six-acre Worcester Common in heart of city. Reflecting pool, crabapple trees, magnolias, black spreading yews. Flower bed quadrangle has several hundred Europeana and Spartan rose bushes planted by the Worcester Garden Club and area 4-H clubs, spring-flowering bulbs and annuals.

YARMOUTH PORT

Captain Bangs Hallet House, Strawberry Lane. Early eighteenth century sea captain's house, owned by the Historic Society of Old Yarmouth. Land consists of fifty-three acres with botanic trails leading to trees, shrubs and wild flowers. Open mid-June to mid-September. Admission.

NEW HAMPSHIRE

State flower, purple lilac. State tree, paper (white) birch.

ALLENSTOWN

Bear Brook State Park, three miles east of center, ninety-three hundred acres of heavily forested land has an Audubon Society Nature Center, offering free programs and displays during July and August. Nature trails.

CRAWFORD NOTCH

Crawford Notch State Park, four miles south of Crawford House on Route 302. Ten miles of rugged, natural beauty in a scenic mountain pass with hiking trails through wild flower and native wildlife areas. Open late May to mid-October. Charge.

DURHAM

Jesse Helper Arboretum, University of New Hampshire, Main Street, two hundred lilacs of several species, best viewed May 15–30. See Chapter 2.

FITZWILLIAM

Rhododendron State Park, off Route 119, three miles from center, sixteen acre grove of fifteen foot high rhododendrons protected by sheltering pine forest in two hundred seventy-eight-acre park. Well-marked hiking trails. Late June to Labor Day. Admission.

FRANCONIA NOTCH

The Flume Gorge, ten miles south of Franconia Village, east of Route 3. An eight-hundred-foot natural chasm extending along the flank of Mount Liberty offers closeup views of rare mountain flowers and luxuriant mosses growing from the lava sheets.

LANCASTER

Weeks State Park, three miles south on Route 3. Former mountaintop estate of John W.

Weeks, one-time Secretary of War has a forestry museum and observation tower with views of nearby states. Mid-June to mid-October. Charge.

MONADNOCK REGION

Mountain laurel tour in towns of Temple, Wilton, Lyndeboro, Milford, Mason and Greenfield. Masses of delicate pink and white blossoms line roadsides and stretch into woodlands around the week of June 15.

NEW IPSWICH

Barrett House (1800), Main Street. Small flower garden laid out according to an early plan of a garden in Portsmouth, New Hampshire. Open Tuesday through Saturday 11 A.M. to 5 P.M., mid-June to mid-October. Admission.

NORTH HAMPTON

Fuller Gardens, Willow Avenue. Extensive gardens on estate of the late Governor Alvan T. Fuller of Massachusetts. More than twenty-five hundred roses, perennials, annuals. Open all seasons but winter. Free. See Chapter 5.

NORTH WOODSTOCK

Lost River Reservation, five miles west on Route 112. Some nine hundred acres, maintained by the Society for the Protection of New Hampshire Forests. Extensive nature gardens with more than three hundred varieties of wild flowers, trees, shrubs, ferns and clubmosses. Trail begins at museum. Open mid-May to mid-October. Admission.

PLAINFIELD

Plainfield Wildflower Sanctuary, River Road, off Route 12A. A hardwood slope, field and bank along the Connecticut River, notable for its great variety of wild flowers and ferns in a concentrated area. A property of the New England Wild Flower Society, Inc.

PLYMOUTH

Polar Caves, four miles west on Route 25. Gigantic caves, unusual rock formations, formed by glaciers, in wooded park of about one hundred acres. Nature trails from entrance building lead to series of caves and to a wild garden in ravine. Evergreens, small rock ferns, lichens. A pathway near the Souvenir Shop is bordered with wild flowers, such as trilliums, Canadian mayflower, arbutus. Open mid-May to mid-October. Admission.

PORTSMOUTH

Governor John Langdon Mansion Memorial (1784), 143 Pleasant Street. Former home of a Revolutionary War leader has flower beds created by the Society for the Preservation of New England Antiquities in context of early twentieth century estate landscaping. Long rose arbor. Open weekdays 1 to 5, June 1 to mid-October. Admission.

Moffatt-Ladd House (1763), Market Street. Lawns and flower beds cover more than an acre and a half. Raised flower beds of old-fashioned flowers, herb garden, rose arbors. Open weekdays, 10 to 5, weekends, 2 to 5. Admission. See Chapter 4.

Strawbery Banke, Hancock Street, a village restoration reflecting this seaport's historic past. More than thirty houses and related buildings ranging in time from 1697 to 1825 on ten-acre site. Garden areas include lilacs, orchard, tree farm, shrub nursery and herbs. Open daily May 1 through October 31, 9:30 to 5. Admission.

Thomas Bailey Aldrich Memorial (1790), Court Street. The home of author Aldrich's grandfather and one he described in *The Story of a Bad Boy*. Owned by the Thomas Bailey Aldrich Memorial Association. Small garden of old-fashioned flowers. Open June 15 to September 15, Monday through Saturday, 10 to 5. Admission.

Wentworth Coolidge Mansion, Little Harbor Road. A forty-two-room structure reflecting three periods of New England architecture (1650, 1700, 1750) was the official residence of Benning Wentworth, first governor of the Province of New Hampshire (1741–1766). Large stands of lilacs on the grounds are believed to be among the first brought to this country from England about 1750.

RINDGE

Cathedral of the Pines, Cathedral Road, off Route 124, international shrine and memorial to those who lost their lives in World War II. Simple gardens among tall pines on four hundred-acre knoll. Open May to November. Free. See Chapter 7.

RHODE ISLAND

State flower, violet. State tree, red maple.

BARRINGTON

Llys-Yr-Rhosyn, eleven-acre garden of Mr. and Mrs. Karl P. Jones at 93 Rumstick Road. More than seventy-five hundred roses, about one thousand varieties, more than two hundred clematis, other flowers. Open mid-May to frost. Free. See Chapter 5.

CENTRAL FALLS

Jenks Park, 580 Broad Street, established in 1913, in center of this "city of churches." Rose gardens. Cockscomb in mid-summer make a splash of color.

CRANSTON

Dialogue Garden, Oaklawn Avenue and Spring Lane Road. Garden, dedicated in October, 1968, is a physical symbol of the purpose of the Dialogue Group, an organization encompassing members of several faiths. The significance of the garden design is its circular form, which denotes unity. Research uncovered significant plants from the Old and New Testaments which were suitable to local climate — Russian olive, burning bush, rock spray, scarlet firethorn, rosebay rhododendron. A ten-ton boulder of granite pointing upward is the focal point of the garden. A redwood arbor for meditation is covered with wisteria.

Winsor Azalea Garden, 44 Marden Street, garden of Mr. and Mrs. Ralph T. Winsor. Private garden open to the public for about three weeks in May when azaleas are in bloom. See Chapter 5.

EAST GREENWICH

General James Mitchell Varnum House (1773), 57 Peirce Street. Historic house and garden are maintained by the Continental Ladies. The garden was restored in 1954 by the Warwick Garden Club with spring bulbs, annuals and staple perennials. Open June to October. Free.

GREENE

Greene Herb Gardens, Narrow Lane Road. Two-acre commercial herb gardens, divided in such segments as kitchen dooryard, English, Bible, dye and half moon herb gardens. Herb kitchen and greenhouses open year-around. Gardens May 1 to November 15 daily except Sunday, 1 to 5 p.m.

KINGSTON

University of Rhode Island, Main Street. Gardens and greenhouses open to the public. Annual gardens planted in early May and on display in early July through frost. Perennial section may be seen in early summer. A dwarf ornamental collection of about two hundred dwarf and slow-growing evergreens is labeled with the common and scientific names. A fall flower show is held in late August. Free.

MIDDLETOWN

Norman Bird Sanctuary and Museum, Third Beach Road. A four hundred fifty-acre wildlife preserve with small natural history museum which offers information on what to see on miles of trails. Admission.

Whitehall (1729) Berkeley Avenue. Home of the British philosopher and Anglican bishop, George Berkeley, restored and furnished by the National Society of Colonial Dames in Rhode Island. Side garden of herbs and old-fashioned roses, enclosed by stone walls and hedge. Garden, a project of the Newport Garden Club, has such early roses as Maiden's Blush damask, Rosa Mundi gallica, Rose of Castile damask.

The planting is concentrated on summer-blooming flowers. Open July and August, 10 A.M. to 5 P.M. Admission to house.

NEWPORT

The Breakers, Ochre Point Avenue. Magnificent mansion, built for Cornelius Vanderbilt in 1895 by Richard Morris Hunt, follows the general theme and ornamentation of seventeenth century Italian villas in Genoa and Turin. The eight-acre grounds have fine specimen trees, including a stand of Japanese maples, kingly copper beech, rows of pine oaks and red maples. There are, paralleling the wrought iron fence, broad borders of rhododendron, laurel, dog-

THE BREAKERS, NEWPORT, RHODE ISLAND

wood and other flowering shrubs. A property of the Preservation Society of Newport County. Open May to November. Admission.

Chateau-sur-Mer, Bellevue Avenue. Victorian mansion built in 1852 for William S. Wetmore, who made his fortune in the China trade. Fine specimen trees and rose garden being restored within a semi-circle of evergreen trees. Property of the Preservation Society of Newport County. Open May to November. Admission.

The Elms, Bellevue Avenue. Built in 1901 for Edward J. Berwind of Philadelphia and New York, the extensive grounds have terraces, tea-houses, statues and fountains. Open May to November. Admission. See Chapter 1.

Rosecliff, Bellevue Avenue. Mansion, built in 1902 for Hermann Oelrichs, designed by Stanford White and modeled after the Petit Trianon of Marie Antoinette at Versailles. Extensive grounds include formal rose garden. Property of the Preservation Society of Newport County. Open May to November. Admission.

PROVIDENCE

Brown University, Prospect Street, Japanese garden of rocks, pines, dogwoods, ground cover of exquisite texture and design, created so seasonal changes may be viewed. Accessible from Cushing Street.

Garden for the Blind, behind headquarters of the Rhode Island Association for the Blind at 1058 Broad Street. Flower bed signs and labels in braille in a two-level garden. Open Monday through Friday, 9 to 5. Free. See Chapter 5.

Roger Williams Park, Broad Street. One of the most beautiful municipal parks in the country, it has ten miles of drives in four hundred fifty acres. A Japanese garden is done in typical Ori-

ental fashion. Floral displays, herb garden at the Betsy Williams Cottage. See Chapter 7.

Shakespeare's Head, 21 Meeting Street. Historic residence, built in 1763, includes the Memorial Room and Garden of the Rhode Island Federation of Garden Clubs. Old-fashioned, formal garden with circular beds on two levels includes plantings of herbs, boxwood, dogwood and quince trees. Gardens open free.

Stephen Hopkins House (1743), Benefit Street. The Dirt Gardeners Club of Providence began restoration of the eighteenth century garden in 1955 from a design by the late Alden Hopkins, a direct descendant of the Hopkins family. The garden is entered by descending five stone steps at each end of an eight-foot high retaining wall. This is a parterre garden and its typical geometric design outlined by a brick wall lends an air of formality. The focal point is an old sundial mounted on a slender pedestal in the center square. Around the dial is engraved a quotation by Stephen Hopkins, "A garden that might comfort yield." Free.

Swan Point Cemetery, 585 Blackstone Boulevard. Garden-type cemetery, laid out in 1847, has fifteen miles of roads on two hundred acres. It is notable for its more than three hundred varieties of trees and shrubs. See Chapter 7.

Temple Beth-El Biblical Garden, 70 Orchard Street. Upper patio of temple contains plants of Biblical authenticity. Open daily 9 A.M. to dusk. See Chapter 5.

WESTERLEY

Wilcox Park, Grove Avenue, established in 1888 by Mrs. Stephen Wilcox, covers thirty-two acres adjoining the Memorial and Public Library, whose association owns the area. There are fine water lily gardens with a long season of bloom from July to October. One of the best upright English oaks, almost forty feet tall, is in the park.

WICKFORD

Smith's Castle (1679), opposite State Police Barracks on Route 1. House in which Roger Williams, the state's founder, preached to the Indians. The eighteenth century garden was planned by the South County Garden Club in 1953 and its design brought the club the coveted Founder's Fund Award of the Garden Clubs of America, which made possible its construction. The garden is not a restoration, but a re-creation of what might have been there. All plant materials are from eighteenth century listings, although in some cases the varieties now available have had to be used. You will find some of the old roses, such as the cabbage, the moss, the rose of Damascus, as well as perennials, such as early peonies, gas plant dittany and the spicy garden pink, annuals including the fragrant cherry pie, pot marigolds and the globe amaranth, and herbs in great variety. Open daily except Thursdays from 10 A.M. to 5 P.M. and Sundays, 1 P.M. to 5 P.M. year around. Admission.

WYOMING

Meadowbrook Herb Garden, on Route 138 a mile east of Interstate 95. More than two hundred culinary, medicinal and ornamental herb varieties grown in greenhouses, outdoor formal gardens and fields. Culinary herbs are harvested and processed into herb seasonings, which are displayed with a variety of herb teas, in the herb shop attached to the greenhouses. Garden and shop open daily from 1 to 6 P.M.

VERMONT

State flower, red clover. State tree, sugar maple.

BURLINGTON

Experiment Station, University of Vermont, South Prospect Street. Greenhouses, trial beds of annuals, perennials, roses. Herbs and ferns may be seen in the *Pringle Herbarium* in the Williams Science Hall.

HANCOCK

Texas Falls Interpretive Trail, three miles west on Route 125 to Route 39 and follow signs, a four-mile marked trail ending with a view of Texas Falls. The trail, on a minute part of the Green Mountain National Forest, pinpoints such growth as witch hobble, lichen, maple trees and hemlock. Within the two hundred forty thousand acre national forest is the *Long Trail*, a wilderness footpath traversing the ridges of the main range of the Green Mountains for two hundred sixty miles, from Massachusetts to Canada.

MANCHESTER

Southern Vermont Art Center, off West Street. This active art center on three hundred seventy-five acres has a Botany Trail, a conservation project of the Garden Club of Manchester, with trees and plants identified, and natural gardens around its Georgian-style house and galleries. Trees, ferns and wild flowers. Open June to mid-October, except Mondays. Admission.

MONTPELIER

State House (1859), State Street. Park around State House, which is built of Vermont granite, covers three acres with gravel paths crossing the lawns and a wide stone walk flanking the flower beds in the center. One of these consists of rose bushes donated by Mrs. Lyndon B. Johnson during the National Beautification Program she engaged in while First Lady. There are lilac bushes bordering the walks, many sugar maples, the State tree, and evergreens. A giant elm tree has a plaque near it, indicating the tree to be the offspring of the elm tree in Cambridge, Massachusetts, under which General George Washington took command of the American Army.

NORTH BENNINGTON

The Governor McCullough Mansion (1865), West Street and Park Street. Former Victorian home of John G. McCullough, Governor of Vermont in 1902, with well-groomed lawns and gardens. Open July through October, Tuesdays through Fridays, Sundays and holidays. Admission. See Chapter 6.

PEACHAM

Stoddard Swamp, three miles west of center, very rough walking and impossible to avoid stepping on rare plants unless accompanied by someone who knows not only the area well but also all unmarked paths. Woodland and bog area, known for its native orchids, is a property of the New England Wild Flower Society, Inc.

SHAFTSBURY

Tapping Tavern Museum, East Road. An eighteenth century stagecoach tavern, outbuildings, pond, views of Green Mountains. Gardens consist of beds and borders of annuals, perennials, some shrubs. Former summer home of Earl and Countess of Gosford. May 1 to October 31, daily except Monday. Admission.

SHELBURNE

Shelburne Museum, one mile south on Route 7. An enchanting community of living Americana, with historic houses, barns, covered bridge moved from many points throughout New England. The museum on forty-five acres has thirty-five buildings filled with art works, craft exhibits and a wide range of artifacts covering three centuries of American life. Gardens include a fifty by fifty foot herb garden planted with the medicinal and culinary herbs that were in common use in the eighteenth and nineteenth centuries. A smaller similar herb garden is planted along the walkway that leads to the old Apothecary Shop. The oldest house on the museum grounds is the Prentis House, circa 1733, from Hadley, Massachusetts. Just south of it is a rose garden planted with three dozen old rose varieties. A few yards away in the direction of the *S.S. Ticonderoga* is an azalea garden. The Circus Parade Building has a four hundred eighty-foot rock garden as a foundation planting. Behind this building are planted four hundred crab apple trees. In addition, the grounds exhibit another eighty apple trees, eight hundred rose bushes, some four hundred French lilacs, spring daffodils, and hollyhocks. Open May 15 through October 15. Admission.

STRAFFORD

Justin Smith Morrill Homestead (1848–1851), south of Common. Historic home of United States Senator Morrill is planted with annuals, perennials, shrubs. Open June 15 to September daily except Monday. State owned.